Lessons from a Translingual Romance

Jieun Kiaer • Hyejeong Ahn

Lessons from a Translingual Romance

Conflict and Cultural Innovation of Intercultural Couples

Jieun Kiaer
Oriental Institute
University of Oxford
Oxford, UK

Hyejeong Ahn
Melbourne Graduate School
of Education
Univesity of Melbourne
Parkville, Australia

ISBN 978-3-031-32920-3   ISBN 978-3-031-32921-0 (eBook)
https://doi.org/10.1007/978-3-031-32921-0

© The Author(s) 2023
This work is subject to copyright. All rights are solely and exclusively licensed by the Publisher, whether the whole or part of the material is concerned, specifically the rights of translation, reprinting, reuse of illustrations, recitation, broadcasting, reproduction on microfilms or in any other physical way, and transmission or information storage and retrieval, electronic adaptation, computer software, or by similar or dissimilar methodology now known or hereafter developed.
The use of general descriptive names, registered names, trademarks, service marks, etc. in this publication does not imply, even in the absence of a specific statement, that such names are exempt from the relevant protective laws and regulations and therefore free for general use.
The publisher, the authors, and the editors are safe to assume that the advice and information in this book are believed to be true and accurate at the date of publication. Neither the publisher nor the authors or the editors give a warranty, expressed or implied, with respect to the material contained herein or for any errors or omissions that may have been made. The publisher remains neutral with regard to jurisdictional claims in published maps and institutional affiliations.

This Palgrave Macmillan imprint is published by the registered company Springer Nature Switzerland AG.
The registered company address is: Gewerbestrasse 11, 6330 Cham, Switzerland

Prologue

This book is an accessible exploration of intercultural couples and their experiences, based on the case studies of 21 couples. Taking Asian-Western couples as our main focus, as well as some Asian-Asian couples, we hope to update this field of study to reflect the diversity of the intercultural couple population. We do not profess to hold all the solutions to the issues that intercultural couples face; rather we will look at a selection of problems and challenges that our interviewees face on a case-by-case basis. In doing so, readers will understand the plurality of experiences that our intercultural couples have had, as well as the issues that arise most often.

We explore intercultural couples through the framework of *translanguaging*, that is to say, how they mix language and culture in a borderless manner. Translanguaging does not just happen between the spouses of an intercultural couple, but also with their children, in-laws, friends, and wider families. This is an emerging area of study to which we wish to contribute. Parents-in-law in particular pose an issue for our Asian-Western couples, as one's relationship with a parent-in-law in Asia is very different to that in the West. All our couples are based in Singapore. Were they to be based in the UK, for example, they might face totally different issues. The way an intercultural couple develops their language practices varies according to where the couple settles.

We also add to the field by considering the significance of technological advancements for our intercultural couples. Before the age of the smartphone and internet, one or both spouses in the intercultural couple would be cut off from their families, only able to call them for short periods of time on unreliable long-distance connections. Both authors remember the painful process of buying phone cards to speak with our family in Korea. In the present day, however, we make a video call and instant message our families at the touch of a screen. Intercultural couples can also quickly use online translation software to resolve any miscommunication issues that they might have. In this way, intercultural couples' experiences have been transformed by the technological developments of the past decade. We update this area of study to take this into account.

Ultimately, we find that it is crucial for both halves of the couple to make an effort to understand each other's cultural and linguistic differences. Belonging to an intercultural couple can never be a one-directional process. It is all about exchange, sharing, negotiation, and adaptation. Each intercultural couple creates their own unique shared culture and language that goes beyond the cultural and linguistic borders of nation states. This book endeavours to share some of their experiences, highlighting the importance of location, in-laws, technology, and diversity.

This book:

- Is a case study based on interviews with 21 intercultural couples, 11 Asian-Western couples, and nine Asian-Asian couples, all of whom live in Singapore
- Provides an easy-to-read exploration of intercultural couples' experiences, exploring issues on a case-by-case basis
- Takes a holistic approach to consider neglected aspects such as the role of in-laws, technology, and location, rather than purely focusing on linguistic aspects

Acknowledgements

We are grateful, first and foremost, to our participants, Andreas, Ayu, Bill, Chris, Christian, Cristina, Dhillon, Dongwook, Emma, Fawn, Fenella, Gideon, Ian, Jamie, Javier, Jim, Judy, Lisa, Mansoo, Mihoko, Priscilla, Rachel, Seonghwan, Sofia, Tiffany, Tim, Yvonne, and many others who wish their names to be anonymised. These participants' identities are protected by using pseudonyms in this manuscript. Without their insightful comments, and their willingness to share their life stories, this project would not have been possible.

We are very grateful to Louise Hossien for her valuable help at every stage of this book. We also owe a great debt to Marc Yeo Fei for assisting with data collection and Susanna Carter for carefully editing this book. We would also like to express our deep gratitude to the many reviewers for their constructive feedback on our research.

A sincere acknowledgement must also be given to our families, Ian, Sarah, Jessie, Martin, and Mason, for their support and encouragement in completing this book. We would also like to acknowledge the School of Humanities at Nanyang Technological University in Singapore for their funding to support our research.

Throughout the book, the use of the first-person pronoun in anecdotes refers to the first author, unless otherwise specified.

This work was supported by the Core University Program for Korean Studies of the Ministry of Education of the Republic of Korea and Korean Studies Promotion Service at the Academy of Korean Studies (AKS-2021-OLU-2250004).

Contents

1 **Intercultural Relationships** 1
  Love Across the Borders 1
  Havens of Translanguaging: Home and the Community 5
  Previous Studies 6
  Intercultural, Cross-Cultural, and Inter-Discourse
  Communication 6
  Translanguaging, Code-Switching, and Code-Mixing 8
  Why Do we Enter an Intercultural Relationship? 10
  The Role of Culture in an Intercultural Relationship 11
  Culture-Related Stressors 11
  Coping Strategies 13
  Communication and Language Choice 14
  Language Choices in Emotional Communication 15
  Methodology 17
  Translanguaging: A Tool for Enabling Intercultural Couples 26
  Structure 29
  References 31

2 **Language Negotiation** 39
  Learning Together: He Had to Force himself to Speak Chinese 40
  Translanguaging: Because It's Showing Respect to his Culture
  and Where he Comes from 43
  Translanguaging: We Sometimes Text in Norwegian 45

Making Do with One Language: I Think he Can, but he Prefers Not to	48
Living for Such a Long Time with me and he Is Not Able to Speak Chinese: It's Really Bad	49
Language of Texting: He Replies in English or in Romanised Korean	51
We Use Pinyin	53
We Can Use the Short Form	53
Summary	54
Reference	54

3 Language of Emotion — 55

The 3 E Model	56
Translanguaging Competence	57
Language of Anger: Completely in English	58
When We Argue, of Course We Argue in English	59
When He Starts Speaking in Chinese that Means He's Okay	60
I Need Chinese to Express	60
I Swear in Slovak	61
Language of Resolution: He'll Start Sending Me Texts	62
Language of Expression: We Lose the Expressive Capacities	63
Language of (In)Expression	64
Language of Affection: If I Want to Be Sweet, I Would Say Some Words in Italian	65
Speaking in Korean when Trying to Wake Him up Makes it Feel a Bit Softer	66
Language of Jokes: Only to Be Cheeky	67
Language of Home: The Language of Cuddles and Putting Them to Sleep	67
Culture and Emotion	69
Summary	70
References	70

4 Language with the Wider Family — 71

Asia, It's All about the Family	73
Meeting the In-Laws	74
Addressing the In-Laws: He Uses 'Eomma', 'Appa', but I Never Called His Parents 'Mom 'Dad'	76

I Don't Call Them Anything	77
I Call Her Mummy	78
Communicating with the In-Laws: He Makes a Lot of Effort to Speak in Slovak	79
They Can't Drop the Subtle Hints	79
There Are Times when Colin Is Rude to Them	81
Living with In-Laws	81
The Miracle of Technology	83
Communicating with In-Laws: If I Had a Local Mother-in-Law, She Probably Won't Be So Expressive	84
Naming Children	85
My Mother Gave Her the Name. I Hated that Name	86
Sometimes My Wife Would Worry about How They Would Be Perceived Overseas	87
A Cross-Cultural Relationship Gave us a Free Pass	88
Talking with Children	89
It's a Small Language, so It's Not So Important	90
It's Mostly for Them to Learn about the Culture	91
They Could Easily Lose Their Chinese Heritage	92
Translanguaging	93
Talking with Friends: We're Just Going to Ignore Him and Speak in Indonesian	94
Otherwise, I Will Feel Like a Burden	95
The Language Is Fun and Dynamic and Fast Moving	95
Summary	96
Reference	97
5 The Language of Culture	**99**
The Landscapes of our Tables	100
Food: Chicken Curry Paella	101
My Idea of Healthy Food Is Western Food	102
Korean Is Actually Only for Food	103
Festivals: He Doesn't Celebrate Anything	104
I'm Just Celebrating by Myself	105
Weddings: An Indonesian Wedding Is More about the Community	106
I Just Feel Like It's like Training a Monkey	108
Gift Giving: Koreans Are more Thoughtful	109

Ideology: We Rarely Have Those Discussions Now 110
He Wouldn't Expect Me to Like, You Know, Serve him and Take Care of Him 111
Let Me Remind you, I'm Not a Mail Order Bride 111
It Always Helps to Remind Me that There's Another Way to Think 112
I don't Even Feel that we Are from Different Contexts 113
Finance: We Are on a more Equal Footing 114
Summary 114
Reference 115

Epilogue 117

References 119

Index 127

ABBREVIATIONS

FLA Foreign Language Anxiety
IC   Intercultural couple
L1   First language
L2   Secondary language
LX   Any language acquired after the L1

CHAPTER 1

Intercultural Relationships

Abstract What is the language of love? In intercultural relationships, language is an important basis on which two people build intimacy. Taking the time to learn another person's language can show love for them, although sacrificing your language for your partner's language can similarly show love too. Love also goes beyond language. Intercultural couples make a lifetime commitment to understanding and learning from each other. This is true not only of each partner's language, but also of their culture. Although every couple will experience different challenges, intercultural couples may experience more challenges on a daily basis, be this in terms of food, clothing, interactions, words, or behaviour. Even everyday mundane tasks require intercultural understanding. On the one hand, cultural differences can enrich a relationship, as both partners learn about different customs. On the other hand, cultural differences can create tension and conflict.

Love Across the Borders

What is the language of love? In intercultural relationships, language is an important basis on which two people build intimacy. Taking the time to learn another person's language can show love for them, although sacrificing your language for your partner's language can similarly show love too. Love also goes beyond language. Intercultural couples make a lifetime

© The Author(s), under exclusive license to Springer Nature Switzerland AG 2023
J. Kiaer, H. Ahn, *Lessons from a Translingual Romance*,
https://doi.org/10.1007/978-3-031-32921-0_1

commitment to understanding and learning from each other. This is true not only of each partner's language, but also of their culture. Although every couple will experience different challenges, intercultural couples may experience more challenges on a daily basis, be this in terms of food, clothing, interactions, words, or behaviour. Even everyday mundane tasks require intercultural understanding. On the one hand, cultural differences can enrich a relationship, as both partners learn about different customs. On the other hand, cultural differences can create tension and conflict.

Misunderstanding between intercultural couples is inevitable. This can occur between couples who speak the same mother tongue, and they occur even more frequently between those who have different linguistic competencies and cultural backgrounds. Patience is key in these situations. If an intercultural couple use English as their main everyday language, as many couples do, then those with a better understanding of English need to be patient with those who are less confident. Processing and computation of information in another language is not easy, and thus a partner might just need more time. This applies not only to discussion but also to humour. Sometimes, nuanced meanings or jokes fail in intercultural interactions because of different language and cultural understanding. This affects not only the two people in the couple but also their daily interactions with their children, wider family, friends, and society. It is for this reason that intercultural communication is key. Intercultural couples need to be open-minded and patient with each other. It is a case of working with what your partner has, rather than asking them to change. Each partner in a couple does not necessarily start on an equal footing, and thus consideration and compromises must be made.

This book looks at 21 intercultural couples, of whom 11 are Asian-Western couples and nine are Asian-Asian couples. Most of them were living in Singapore at the time of interview. We will be looking at how intercultural interaction enables our couples to have enriched relationships, and how this can lead to cultural conflict too. In looking at this relatively understudied demographic, we will see how Asian and Western societal norms impact their relationships. Asian societies tend to place a lot of value on hierarchy, be that in terms of age, occupation, or wealth, whilst Western societies favour a less hierarchical style of interaction. Very often, Asian hierarchical relationships clash with Western-style relationships. Such clashes happen not only between spouses, but also with in-laws and wider family.

Although intercultural couples have been studied, this book brings the voices of Asian-Western intercultural couples to the forefront. We provide interview data as the main basis of evidence. We look at how intercultural communication is not just an issue of words, but of the non-verbal too. How you say something can be more important than what you say. The cultural context in which you say something can also hold more weight than the exact words that you use. For example, silence in Asian cultures can be a sign of attentive listening, whilst it can be a sign of disinterest in the West. In the West, eye contact is often a sign of attentive listening, yet in many Asian cultures, it can be seen as rude. In Bulgaria shaking one's head is a common sign of agreement, as it is in Greece, Iran, Lebanon, Turkey* and Egypt, whilst other countries commonly see it as meaning 'no'. This book gives a platform for intercultural couples' voices, emphasising the non-verbal elements of intercultural negotiation, as well as the verbal elements. Rather than being a generalisation that proposes to solve all the problems of intercultural couples, this book is a small case study, touching only on heterosexual relationships, that offers new insights on intercultural couples for our readers to take into consideration.

As social mobility has become more prevalent, immigration is on the rise, and so are intercultural relationships. Large-scale waves of immigration across Asia began in the nineteenth century. Between 1840 and 1940, 20 million people from China and 30 million people from India migrated to the growing cities and plantations of Southeast Asia (Amrith, 2014). In the 1960s, there was immigration from Korea and the Philippines to Vietnam to build US military installations during the Vietnam War. At around the same time, people from all over Asia began to migrate to Australia, Canada, New Zealand, and the US. Since 2005, the number of immigrants to Singapore has grown from 1.7 million to 2.5 million, which is almost half of the country's total population (Hirschmann, 2022). The immigrant population is largely made up of Asians, with Malaysian, Chinese, and Indonesian immigrants making up a large share (Hirschmann, 2021). In 2017, over one in four marriages were between one person who was a resident of Singapore and one who was a non-resident. This means that over one quarter of marriages in Singapore are transnational, explaining why it is so pertinent to study intercultural couples in Singapore.

Both the authors of this book are Korean. Jieun is married to a British man while Hyejeong is married to an Australian man. This book is very close to us and the communities that we live in. For instance, Jieun is surrounded by intercultural couples in her neighbourhood. In one family that she knows, Irene is from Catalonia and Theo is from Denmark. Because of this, their son Luke can speak Danish and Catalan, although he speaks mainly English when he goes to nursery. Their family speaks more than three languages on a daily basis, though mainly English. Because of their family history, their version of English is a little bit different from the Kiaer family's, as they mix Spanish, Catalan, and Danish words into their English. Jieun's other neighbours, Henry and Tess, are from Hungary and the Philippines respectively. Tess's family is originally from the Philippines, but they moved to Los Angeles when Tess was a young girl. Tess then moved to the UK. Henry used to live in Budapest and speaks Hungarian and English, while Tess speaks English with a bit of Tagalog. Their son, Lorenzo, speaks English in nursery but can also speak and understand a bit of Tagalog and Hungarian, which he uses when they visit his grandparents. For Jieun's neighbours, English is the language that binds everyone in the family together; however, it is not necessarily the language that each member, particularly the parents, finds the most comfortable or familiar. Families like these exist all over the globe. Over the past 20 years, the percentage of students in UK schools whose first language is not English has almost doubled. In 2002, 10% of pupils spoke English as an additional language (National Association for Language Development In the Curriculum, NALDIC, n.d.). As of 2021, 19.3% of pupils have been reported to have a first language other than English (UK Department of Education 2022). This means that, going forward, many relationships will require the negotiation of multiple cultures and languages.

The borders between languages and nation states are more blurred than ever before, and so it is more important than ever to deepen our understanding of intercultural couples. We need to acknowledge that intercultural relationships have their ups and downs. In doing so, we can start to create an environment with a healthier understanding of intercultural couples and their needs. This will benefit their children and wider family too, which can only have a positive impact on our society. In the Western world, there is a history of marginalisation and lack of appreciation for Asian people. Echoes of this can be seen even now with the rise of Asian hate and xenophobia. Such discrimination stems from a lack of understanding, which creates tension, which then develops into hate. Better intercultural understanding is thus needed to curb such thinking.

Havens of Translanguaging: Home and the Community

Sometimes we think immigrants can (and even should) adapt and learn new languages without any problems. Yet, Sevinc and Backus (2019) have found that immigrants suffer from Foreign Language Anxiety, and that 'there is a vicious circle that connects bilinguals' language knowledge, language use and language anxiety' (p. 706). Li (2011) first coined the term *translanguaging space* to refer to 'a space for the act of translanguaging as well as a space created through translanguaging', where people with multiple linguistic and cultural repertoires feel comfortable shifting creatively between repertoires and asserting their full linguistic identity. Following Li's work (2011), which addressed translanguaging primarily in social spaces within educational spheres (e.g. universities or weekend Chinese schools), several studies have begun to explore further types of 'translanguaging spaces'. Zhu, Li, and Lyons (2017), for instance, discuss the multi-modality of translingual space in a Polish shop in London. Mazzaferro (2018) presents examples of diverse settings where translanguaging can be used in daily practice. Most recently, Kiaer et al. (2022) examine a range of translanguaging spaces, including 'personal', 'philosophical', and 'playful' spaces. Perhaps most pertinent to this book is Kiaer (2021), who refers to a 'safe translanguaging space' in a study that demonstrates how ethnic minority community centres play the role of a 'home away from home' for ethnic minority diaspora by providing a linguistically safe translanguaging space. The home is also a 'safe space' for ICs. Immigrant spouses can feel disconnected from their roots. Moving to another country can feel like becoming a child and having to learn to navigate the adult world all over again. Home should be a space that is safe for an immigrant spouse, and a space in which they can feel at ease. Home is, at the very least, somewhere that immigrant spouses can communicate without feeling judged about their language. More than this, however, home should be a space where ICs innovate something beyond just one culture or the other. It should be a hybrid space in which all cultural heritages can exist. In taking the time to negotiate this transcultural space, spouses show care for each other. This can help immigrant spouses to feel less frustrated and isolated. For spouses whose mother tongue is not the dominant language of the society in which they live, this space is vital for their linguistic and psychological well-being.

Previous Studies

Scholarly and media interest in the issues of intercultural and interracial marriage is not a new phenomenon. However, intercultural and interracial couples in the past and at present have not always been perceived positively and are often considered a deviation from the norm of conventional couples. This is evident from many legal documents, such as the Nazis' infamous Nuremberg laws and South Africa's apartheid. Intercultural and interracial marriages were illegal in most areas of the US until the 1960s. In 1967, Richard and Mildred Loving successfully challenged the constitutionality of the ban on interracial marriage in Virginia. Their case reached the US Supreme Court as Loving v. Virginia. The Supreme Court voted unanimously in Richard's favour, citing the ban against interracial marriage as unconstitutional under the equal protection and due process clauses of the Fourteenth Amendment.

What might have been seen as an abnormal choice for our parents' and grandparents' generations has now become far from unconventional. With the boundaries of ethnicity and race becoming more and more blurred, more people are establishing intercultural partnerships (Lee & Bean, 2004). As a result, there is increased complexity around how to define couples from different racial, cultural, and/or linguistic backgrounds. In some countries, couples might identify as intercultural if they come from different class backgrounds or if they are from the same ethnic background but grew up in different countries. For example, in India, the term intercultural refers to relationships where the partners come from different caste backgrounds and communities.

In this book, we will review contested terms that are common in the studies of intercultural relationships. We will then review studies identifying issues that are key parts of an intercultural relationship. Then, the primary focus of intercultural relationship studies will be discussed, including the impact of cultural differences on intercultural relationships and factors that cause conflict, such as food choice, parenting style, and educational issues. Finally, we will explore studies of the language choices that couples make during disputes and intimate emotional communication.

Intercultural, Cross-Cultural, and Inter-Discourse Communication

Scholars from various disciplines have employed numerous terms to refer to couples made up of different cultural groups. In linguistics, terms such as *bilingual couples* or *multilingual couples* are often used when the focus of a study is couples' language use. When cultural aspects are examined, terms such as *bicultural*, *cross-cultural*, and *intercultural* are commonly applied. Scollon and Scollon (2001), who adopted the discourse approach to investigate the communication of intercultural couples, clarified the differences between the three terms, *cross-cultural communication*, *intercultural communication*, and *inter-discourse communication*. The term *cross-cultural communication* is used when comparing communicative interactions amongst people of the same culture to those from another. *Intercultural communication* refers to communicative interactions between people from different cultures. While both terms are based on the assumption that there are distinct cultural groups, the term *inter-discourse communication* sees culture as a discursively constructed discourse and avoids the arbitrarily defined concept of 'culture'. *Inter-discourse communication* is defined as communication across discourse systems. The discourse system here refers to 'any group that has particular ways of thinking, treating other people, communicating and learning that can be said to be participating in a particular discourse system' (Scollon et al., 2012, p. 8).

As inter-discourse communication scholars rightly acknowledge, the concept of culture has been widely contested; multiple definitions exist and are the topic of debate. The term 'culture' can evoke different meanings for different people. Its meaning may be affected by factors such as gender, class, ethnicity, social difference, and background. Kroeber and Kluckhohn (1963) collected 156 definitions of 'culture'. Since then, more than six decades have passed, and scholarly and media interest in intercultural studies has increased considerably. Culture can refer to a 'national asset', 'social heritage', 'art', and 'festivals', also called 'high culture'. There is also 'low culture', generally referring to popular culture. Culture is also seen as values (beliefs, common understandings), norms (a set of rules), and practices assumed to be shared by a group with which individuals identify.

Furthermore, categorising a cultural group is also a highly complex and discursive task. Finding answers to what distinguishes one cultural group from another may not be straightforward. The definition of what constitutes a cultural group can be fluid and change significantly over time. People tend to have their own ideas about how their culture or cultural group is distinct from other groups. Therefore, our study relies on participants' perceptions of culture and the cultural differences between them and their partners, instead of applying scholarly defined concepts to interpret participants' perceived cultures.

Translanguaging, Code-Switching, and Code-Mixing

Another key concept that needs to be defined is 'translanguaging', which has received considerable academic attention in recent years (Canagarajah, 2013; Canagarajah, 2011; Canagarajah & Dovchin, 2019; García & Li, 2014; Lee, 2022; Lee & Canagarajah, 2021; Li, 2018). While *translanguaging* has a range of definitions, two studies that captured most attention in the bilingual and multilingual field are Li (2011) and García and Leiva (2014), who wrote:

> Translanguaging is both going between different linguistic structures and systems, including different modalities (speaking, writing, singing, listening, reading, remembering) and going beyond them. It includes the full range of linguistic performances of multilingual language users for purposes that transcend the combination of structures, the alternation between systems, the transmission of information and the representation of values, identities and relationships. (Li, 2011, p. 1223)

> Translanguaging is related to other fluid languaging practices that scholars have called by different terms…But what makes translanguaging different from these other fluid languaging practices is that it is transformative, attempting to wipe out hierarchy…Thus, translanguaging could be a mechanism for social justice, especially when teaching students from language minoritised communities. (García & Leiva, 2014, p. 200)

Translanguaging moves away from the concept of named languages and tries to identify the fluid process by which different linguistic systems are utilised by multilinguals.

Before further discussing the concept of 'translanguaging', it is necessary to review two widely (mis)used terms, 'code-mixing' and 'code-switching'. Traditionally, these two terms are applied to describe the multilingual speech context. Code-switching generally refers to the inter-sentential mixing of code, whereas code-mixing refers to intra-sentential mixing (Gumperz & Gumperz, 1981; Milroy & Gordon, 2003; Moyer, 1997; Myers-Scotton, 1993; Tay, 1989). Code-switching involves blending words, phrases, or sentences from two languages across sentence boundaries. Thus, it requires fairly advanced competence in both languages, meaning it is a common language practice among bilingual speakers (Moyer, 1997). There are two types of code-switching: situational code-switching and metaphorical code-switching (Gumperz, 1982).

Situational code-switching occurs when the situation changes, such as participants, setting, and activity type, including argumentative or affective moments. Metaphorical code-switching happens when speakers aim to achieve special communicative effects.

In comparison, code-mixing involves mixing various smaller linguistic units (i.e. morphemes, words, phrases, clauses) within the same sentence. Thus, it does not necessarily require proficient bilingual skills. Many studies also look at the motivations and communicative effects of code-mixing and code-switching, such as marking reiteration, emphasis, accomplishing repair, enhancing turn selection, contextualising topic changes, and softening refusal (Gibbons, 1987; Gumperz, 1982; Muysken, 2000; Tay, 1989). In more recent studies, code-switching and code-mixing have also been reported to express modernity and luxury and to generate humorous effects in the Korean context (Ahn, 2017; Kim, 2006). However, the limitations of the two terms have been consistently addressed and documented, including difficulties in defining 'borrowed words', 'hybridised expressions', and 'code', which are all prevalent linguistic practices in multilingual speech contexts (Li, 2018, p. 27).

These terms are contested by many scholars, who argue that they give a 'picture of whole languages added one on top of the other to form multilingual practices' (Canagarajah, 2013, p. 7). They connote different language groups where multilingual speakers consciously or subconsciously select one language over another (i.e. code-switching or code-mixing) to occupy their own communicative niche. Although Canagarajah (2013) does not reject the presence of named languages, he views languages as historically, politically, and ideologically defined entities. Thus, multilinguals are aware of the existence of these contextually loaded languages, and they have the ability to use them when required. From a translanguaging perspective, asking simply which languages are being used, mixed, and borrowed is an unexciting and insignificant question. The notion of translanguaging does not aim to describe or analyse fluid forms of multilingualism but to explain a process and practice involving dynamic knowledge construction that goes beyond the named language(s) (Li, 2018).

Although these reviewed terms may have different theoretical and practical orientations, the present study will adopt the most commonly used term, *intercultural couple*, when referring to the participants in this study, but when referring to their language practices, the term *translingual* will be adopted, where appropriate.

Why Do we Enter an Intercultural Relationship?

Piller (2009) identified the interlinked and multifaceted desires that motivate people to enter intercultural relationships from a linguistic perspective. These factors include 'language desire', that is, the desire to master another language, a desire for access to interactional partners in the target language, a desire for one's children to become fluent bilinguals, and a desire to become a legitimate member of another language community. Language desire is often associated with the discourse and ideologies portrayed by media or stereotypical presentations of a particular country or language. This includes the dominance of the English language as the global lingua franca and the language of power, persistent myths about native English speaker status, and the value attached to bilingualism and internationalisation.

In addition to Piller's identification of language desire, the desires for social and financial security have often been discussed by scholars in sociology. Constable (2003, 2005) and Fu and Heaton (2000) look at intercultural couples with vastly different socio-economic backgrounds, particularly the couples in the discourse of 'mail order brides' or 'mail order marriages'. Filipina and Chinese women who meet their Western partners through a 'mail order' marriage agency are primarily motivated by finding a 'ticket out of poverty' for them and their family (Constable, 2003). Because of the economic motivation behind such marriages, wives who are labelled as 'mail order brides' appear to be unfairly represented and suffer from negative public discourse.

Media-portrayed stereotypes have been known to aggravate conflict for intercultural couples. Particularly if the intercultural relationship is established on cultural stereotypes, partners can interact with unrealistic expectations (Coupland et al., 1991; Molina et al., 2004; Taweekuakulkit, 2005). Taweekuakulkit (2005) provided several examples of North American views of Southeast Asian women as quiet, submissive, uncomplaining, and eager to serve because of the reinforcement of this view by their mass media. Some publications, like *Sarong Party Girls*, by Cheryl Lu-Lien Tan (2016), feature Singaporean girls who exclusively date *'ang moh-* rich Westerner expats'. Such media presents these women as wearing provocative clothing and being readily available sexually, which only serves to add to the stereotype. Skowroński et al. (2014) note that intercultural couples with an *ang moh* partner in Singapore feel worried about negative judgements from society, which adds conflict and unnecessary stress to the relationship.

The Role of Culture in an Intercultural Relationship

Culture is a hard word to define. Nonetheless, the fact that culture impacts on the concepts of love and marriage and how individuals feel, think, and behave in close relationships has been readily agreed upon (Kline et al., 2008). For example, love in India is conceptualised in romantic emotions and commitment to each other and members of the wider family (Kashyap, 2020). Abela et al. (2020) address the impact of culture on intercultural relationships from a family therapy perspective. They examine intercultural couples who are from and live in various cultural contexts, including countries from regions as diverse as Scandinavia, the Arab region, France, Malta, China, and India. Abela et al. demonstrate that there are distinctive cultural impacts on intimate relationships and discuss how 'love' can be defined differently from culture to culture. Research in this area has also focused on intercultural couples who are simultaneously living in two or more cultures and the impact of cultural differences on relationships. Tien (2013) found that cultural differences and language differences represented half of the themes in interviews with intercultural couples. Especially at the beginning of their relationship, couples tend to focus on getting to know each other, comparing cultures, and being readily available to their new partner (Brahic, 2013). Abela et al. (2020) show how people's beliefs and values are interwoven with their cultural background and how people in an intercultural relationship erroneously dismiss the significant impacts of cultural differences on their relationship.

Culture-Related Stressors

Studies into culture-related stressors experienced by intercultural couples have been widely documented. The intercultural relationship is, in general, known to be at higher risk of experiencing conflict, tensions, stress, dissatisfaction, long-term instability, and a higher probability of separation and divorce compared to those in relationships with partners from the same background (Bratter & King, 2008; Brummett & Steuber, 2015; Zhang & Van Hook, 2009). Bustamante et al. (2011) identified several stressors, including childrearing (parenting) and gender role expectations. They argued that although many of the stressors might be similar to those in a same culture relationship, cultural differences can exacerbate them,

The challenges stemming from having different cultural views on parenting have been studied extensively by many scholars (Bhugun, 2017, 2019; Lawton et al., 2013; Quah, 2003). Bustamante et al. (2011) quoted interview excerpts which realistically present the difficulties associated with childrearing from different cultural backgrounds. One woman is quoted as saying that her husband is '100% opposite' to her. Decisions around education are one of the primary sources of conflict. Lawton et al. (2013) found that husbands who are Asian or Latino are more likely to exercise control on educational issues. Quah (2003) reports on the significant influence of culture on various aspects of parenting style, including methods of discipline, expectations of child behaviour, demonstration of affection, and the roles of parents. Berg-Cross (2001) also noted the challenges associated with divergent styles of parenting, that is, authoritative, authoritarian, permissive, or uninvolved. Furthermore, Cerchiaro (2017) analysed parenting issues related to children's naming practices and argued that naming practices are closely connected with a couple's racial, ethnic, and faith backgrounds, expectations of the family of origin, and the social context.

Regarding challenges associated with gender expectations, Iwakabe (2019) argues that diversity is a relatively new concept in Japan. Japanese intercultural couples tend to encounter issues associated with culturally bound gender roles and the societal pressure to conform to implicit cultural norms. Bustamante et al. (2011) similarly argue that gender expectations were identified in participants from traditionally male-dominated national cultures (Persian, Mexican, Greek, and Colombian). They found that women were expected to take primary responsibility for childrearing and household chores. Tien (2013) also noted the challenges related to culturally expected gender roles, such as the man as the breadwinner.

Many studies have found food and drink-related stress and differences across generations. Rogan et al. (2018) examined intercultural household food tensions using 'relational dialectics analysis' (Baxter, 1987, 2004; Baxter & Montgomery, 1996). Their study reported that 'food' was among the most frequently mentioned challenges amongst intercultural couples. The identified food-related tensions come from disagreements as to what constitutes 'good' food and how to prepare and serve food for special occasions. The study discussed that food consumption could enable the partners to achieve both stability and novelty within their relational culture, pursuing interdependence and autonomy. Similarly, Leeds-Hurwitz (2009) also noted particular challenges faced by intercultural couples associated with ceremonial food preparation and consumption, such as 'how and when a meal should be eaten' and 'where it should be served'. The study also reported that food-related tension is aggravated when extended family members are invited. Rogan et al. (2018) highlight that intercultural couples can achieve a form of balance in food consumption through transitory compromise, and emphasise the importance of acculturation and enculturation theories to understand the unique relational culture around food. Tien (2013) noted that although food can be a source of challenges, it provides a bonding opportunity which can create a hybridised and fusion food culture that their own family only shares privately. An intercultural family's food consumption is an important example of how a hybridised intercultural family identity is constructed in action (Epp et al. 2014).

Shenhav et al. (2016) examined young adults' experiences with intercultural romantic relationships by ethnicity and immigrant generation. They report that Asian participants perceived greater attitudinal discrepancies from their parents towards intercultural dating than did participants from Latino and European backgrounds. In addition, first- and second-generation participants were more likely to experience intercultural dating conflict with parents than third-generation participants.

COPING STRATEGIES

Cultural differences may aggravate the level of relationship stress experienced by intercultural couples. Intercultural couples may face difficulties in maintaining their relationship in a balanced way and are more often in need of seeking intervention and counselling. Social scientists, particularly in the areas of racial and ethnicity studies, family relationships, family therapy, counselling, and psychology, tend to focus on investigating factors sparking conflict in intercultural couples. They suggest coping strategies and publish clinical handbooks for intercultural couples therapy (Falicov, 1995). Seshadri and Knudson-Martin (2013) investigated 17 intercultural and interracial couples and presented strategies to be used in clinical practice, such as ways to create 'we-ness', ways to frame differences in a constructive way, methods to provide emotional support during conflict, and how to cope with familial and societal challenges.

Stępkowska (2021) employs the term 'biculturalism' to explain, accept, and create the linguistic and cultural duality of intercultural couples and their changing perception of themselves and their partners. Biculturalism addresses the juxtaposition of cultural differences with cultural relatedness and cultural distance, and the values and attitudes of transnational and adaptable characters. Many couples in intercultural relationships should see each other as mere individuals rather than different people with stereotypical traits from a particular culture or nation. Bystydzienski (2011) also suggested that accepting differences should be treated as a kind of 'invisible line' which cannot be crossed and with which both partners agree to live (p. 168). Similar findings are also noted in Piller (2007), who states that intercultural couples tend to find that they are less likely to frame themselves as being different from each other as time passes. They deconstruct their differences as the relationship becomes more established. Being involved in an intercultural partnership is not a mere union between two people from different cultural groups but also an intimate bridge in the form of hybridisation between different cultural groups (Kalmijn, 1998).

Another notable piece of literature that examines the influences of cultural differences of ICs and their coping strategies is Bystydzienski's (2011) *Intercultural couples: Crossing Boundaries, Negotiating Difference*. Bystydzienski argues that fostering a 'relational identity' is crucial as it helps couples create accommodative behaviour and plays a significant role in preventing potential conflicts. The book suggests that as intercultural partners can actively construct a relational identity, over time, most become less concerned with cultural differences. Instead, their identities are likely to become increasingly hybridised and related. As the relationship progresses, differences become normalised, with persistent disruptions and challenges hybridised into the couple's daily life (Brahic, 2013). Hybridised cultural normalisation was particularly noted in 'English as lingua franca (ELF) couples' whose shared language is English but neither of the couples' mother tongues. These couples actively hybridise their private communication, which is drawn from their own cultural and linguistic resources (Dervin, 2013). Le Gall and Meintel (2015) addressed a similar notion to Brahic (2013) in that the normalisation of the plural identities of intercultural couples is a positive and effective by-product of an intercultural relationship.

COMMUNICATION AND LANGUAGE CHOICE

That's Not What I Meant! by Deborah Tannen (1986) has attracted significant attention to the centrality of language use in the success of intercultural marriages. Tannen helped bring academic attention to the importance of communication and language choice in intercultural relationships. Later Piller (2002) conducted an empirical study examining the linguistic practices of bilingual and cross-cultural couples of English-speaking and German-speaking backgrounds, using a discourse analytic approach. Piller argues that their bilingual language choices present the couples' hybrid and multiple identities, ideology, and polyphony (referring to the various facets of their language use). Pillier also discusses 'private language' practices, showing how private discourse is constructed within multiple ideologies. A more recent study by Stępkowska (2021) confirms the significance of using private language to project biculturalism and to voice dual identities. It is, however, important to note that there are several factors that motivate language choice, and the language choices of bilingual couples are highly diverse and personal. Therefore, it is critical to resist stereotypes or the generalisation of the language practices of bilinguals.

Language Choices in Emotional Communication

How language choices express emotion has been extensively researched by sociolinguist Jean-Marc Dewaele. Dewaele (2015) examined the language choices made for emotional 'inner speech' and argued that a language learned later in life (LX) is used significantly less for emotional inner speech (Dewaele, 2018b). Even for multilingual speakers who display dominant use of LX, the use of the first language (L1) in emotional situations is not completely wiped out. Multilingual speakers feel L1s have more emotionally laden words for expressing their emotions. LX languages have been associated with weaker emotional connotations (Dewaele, 2013). Nonetheless, Dewaele (2015) also identified that if a particular type of emotion is experienced in the LX, it might be more natural to express this particular emotion in the LX. For example, intimate emotions in an intercultural relationship when experienced in later life in a person's LX are more easily expressed in the LX. Piller (2017) similarly suggests that the language choice for love is closely associated with culturally established norms on the frequency of saying 'I love you'. This indicates that the language chosen for the expression of emotion evolves, as it can be influenced by socialisation in an LX and through interactions with people in their various LXs.

Dewaele and Salomidou (2017) also examine the challenges in emotional communication caused by language and cultural differences. Their study finds that at the beginning of the relationship, partners feel that expressing their emotions in a language other than their L1 somehow does not sound genuine, but this fades as time passes. Longer relationships lead to effective socialisation in the LX. The LX can often become the language of the heart in the couple's relationship. Subsequently, Dewaele (2018a) examined potential factors that cause difficulties in emotional communication for intercultural couples. The study's statistical analysis reported that participants with higher emotional stability, flexibility, open-mindedness, and educational level experience fewer difficulties, as did male participants in general. Dewaele (2018a) also identified some of the causes of challenges in emotional communication, including linguistic and pragmalinguistic issues (i.e. lexical constraint in their LX), misinterpretations of pragmatic expressions, and sociopragmatic issues (i.e. misunderstanding of silence and non-verbal display of emotion). These findings were also supported by other studies (Pietikäinen, 2016; Tien, 2013; Zhu, 2019). Communication difficulties can come from the inability to express oneself fully in a language learned later in life. This can sometimes cause misunderstanding, and couples feel frustrated when the intended meaning is lost in translation.

Chi (2014) examines language choice for the expression of negative emotion during arguments, focusing on language use in the Taiwanese context, using a discourse analysis approach. Chi argues that code-switching is used as a linguistic strategy to mitigate or neutralise disagreement, and as a tactical tool to present dual voices that express feelings of belonging and the desire for distance at the same time. Kull's (2018) study that examines language choices made when expressing 'anger' amongst Estonian and Australian couples reports that anger is often expressed in the L1, which is consistent with previous findings (Dewaele, 2013, 2016, 2018a). The use of the L1, despite advanced proficiency in a later learned language, signals to their partner that they are angry. Language choice for ICs is emotion-specific, where a person may choose one language over another to express a particular emotion.

It has also been agreed that a multilingual couple's language choice can affect power dynamics in the relationship and language expertise can become a source of dispute (Lee, 2005; Rosenblatt, 2011; Takigawa, 2010). Rosenblatt (2011) suggested that sometimes the language which a couple uses most is more likely to be the language of the partner who has more power within the relationship. Lee (2005) investigated asymmetrical linguistic proficiency in Korean-English partnerships and demonstrated that a linguistically proficient partner takes a superior position during a dispute: an English-speaking husband used his advanced linguistic knowledge to correct his wife's English use, which aggravated the Korean wife's linguistic insecurity. The study reported that the Korean wife chose to vent her anger in Korean when she felt frustrated at not being able to fully express her feelings in English. Her venting in Korean gave her a sense of relief, as well as privacy.

Methodology

This book will look at intercultural relationships and the issues that each couple faces. Our findings are based upon interviews with 21 intercultural couples that were conducted virtually on Zoom. Our participants are mostly made up of couples with one Western partner and one Asian partner. Many studies have focused on intercultural couples where both partners are European. Few studies have focused on Asian-Western and Asian-Asian couples, and as such, this book will help to shed light on a relatively underrepresented group.

A participant description of each couple can be found below. For privacy, all names have been changed:

Jane and Tony
Jane is a Chinese national who is ethnically Korean. She grew up speaking Korean and she felt more comfortable speaking in Korean prior to university. She improved her Mandarin language proficiency at university and at work. Now, she speaks Mandarin with her partner, Tony. Tony is a native speaker of English and has experience in learning French before coming to China. Since his arrival in China, he has made a considerable effort to learn Mandarin and his proficiency has been accelerated since meeting his Mandarin-, Korean-, and English-speaking wife, Jane.

Mike and Nayoung
Nayoung is a Korean woman who speaks Korean as her first language. She also speaks English. Mike is French. His first language is French, but he speaks English too. This couple speak English together. Nayoung does not know much French, and Mike does not know much Korean. They have one son with whom they adopt a 'one parent, one language' policy: Nayoung only speaks to him in Korean and Mike only speaks to him in French.

Erika and Marcus
Erika is a native speaker of Slovak, who also speaks English, and some French, Norwegian, and Malay. Marcus is Singaporean. His first languages are English and Mandarin. He also speaks some French, Norwegian, and Slovak. The pair met in a Norwegian class. They mainly speak English together, but they add in French, Norwegian, and Slovak from time to time too. They speak Slovak, English, and Mandarin to their son.

Colin and Aliyah
Aliyah is a Sri Lankan woman who was born in Sri Lanka and then lived in Kuwait from the ages of four to 16 after which she moved to Australia with her family. Colin is an Australian man. The couple met at film school and have been together for 10 years. The couple speak English together, but Aliyah also speaks Sinhalese with their daughter.

Caleb and Rose
Caleb and Rose come from mixed heritages. Caleb's family background includes a mixture of South Asian, Southeast Asian, East Asian, and European heritage. He has Scottish, Malaysian, Portuguese, and Indonesian heritage on his mother's side, and Indian and Chinese heritage on his father's side. Caleb speaks English as his first language, and he has learnt some Malay and Mandarin whilst at work. Rose's father is Indian, and her mother is of Portuguese, Dutch, and Sri Lankan heritage. She also speaks English as her first language, as well as some Tamil. They have one son together.

Farah and Craig
Farah is a native speaker of Bahasa Indonesia, who grew up in Indonesia but now lives in Singapore. Craig is a New Zealander whose mother tongue is English. He has lived in various Asian countries throughout his adult life and has been exposed to other languages and cultures. The couple have two children who are five and eight years old. Farah and Craig speak in English 90% of the time, even though Craig can speak a bit of Bahasa Indonesia. They spoke more Bahasa Indonesia when they were living in Indonesia, but now that they live in Singapore, they have ended up speaking English more frequently.

Nate and Thea

Nate is a native English speaker from Scotland who lives in Singapore. He moved to China for work in 1998, during which time he began to learn Mandarin. His previous partner was Chinese, and he has two sons from that relationship. Thea is a Taiwanese woman who speaks Mandarin as her first language. She studied in the UK and US, and she speaks English too. Nate and Thea have a melded family, comprising Nate and Thea's children from past relationships. They live in Singapore and used to work for the same education company. Thea has two daughters, aged 17 and 14 years and Nate's sons live with them for half of each week. The main language of communication within the household is English.

Luis and Yvette

Yvette is a Cuban woman who moved to Malaysia in her 30s. Whilst living in Cuba, she only spoke Spanish. When she moved to Malaysia, she learnt English for her work. She later moved to Singapore where she met Luis at a salsa dance class. Luis was born in the US. His mother is from Panama and his father is from Chile. He grew up speaking mostly English, and he only knows some conversational Spanish. Yvette and Luis speak English as their main language together, although they use Spanish to communicate with each other's families. Yvette has one daughter from a previous relationship. Luis has two sons from a previous relationship.

Stefan and Yutong
Yutong is a Chinese national and native speaker of Mandarin. Stefan is a German man, and his mother tongue is German. They communicate in English. Yutong studied in the UK and US for her postgraduate studies and has a good command of English. Stefan uses English at work and has lived and worked in the US, and therefore he has a good command of English too. Stefan does not speak Mandarin and Yutong does not speak German. The couple have been married for five years. They have one daughter who is three years old.

Yiyi and Alonso
Yiyi is a Chinese woman who speaks Mandarin and several Chinese dialects. Alonso is an Italian man and native Italian and Piedmontese speaker, which is an Italian dialect. Alonso also speaks some French and German, and he knows Latin and Greek. Alonso has struggled with learning Mandarin, and so the couple speak in English together.

Lucia and Manny
Lucia is a native Spanish speaker who has lived in Singapore for 18 years. She speaks French, English, and Basque. Manny was born in Singapore, after his parents moved there from India in the 1940s. He speaks many of the languages that he has been exposed to whilst growing up in Singapore, such as Mandarin, Malay, Hokkien, and Cantonese. He also speaks some Punjabi because of his family background. The couple live in Singapore together with their son and daughter. They speak English together and Lucia speaks English and Spanish to her children. Her oldest son speaks good Spanish, as she wasn't working full time when he was growing up. Her youngest daughter speaks much less Spanish because Lucia was working full time when she was younger, so she couldn't speak to her as much. Manny speaks some Punjabi with his children. The children also speak Singlish. At home, the family speak in English, using some Spanish, but mostly in a joking way.

Charlie and John

Charlie and John met online as language buddies. Charlie is a Singaporean woman who speaks English, Korean, and Mandarin proficiently. John is a Korean man who speaks Korean and some English. Having never lived outside of Korea, John moved to Singapore to live with Charlie, after they met online. He quit a fairly high-paying job in Korea and has since been struggling to find work in Singapore. Charlie and John speak Korean together, but they speak English with their son.

Evelyn and Sanghoon

Evelyn is a Singaporean woman of Chinese heritage. She speaks English, Mandarin, and Korean. Sanghoon is a Korean man who moved to Singapore for work after graduating from university. The couple have been together for seven years, and they have one daughter. Evelyn and Sanghoon speak a mix of Korean and English together. They speak a mixture of

English and Korean with their daughter also, and Evelyn sometimes speaks to her in Mandarin too.

Manshik and Tallulah
Manshik is a Korean man who moved to Singapore for work. He speaks Korean, English, and Japanese. He went to school in New Zealand and then lived in Japan for two years before moving to Singapore. Tallulah is Chinese Malaysian. English is her main language, but she speaks Chinese at home with her parents and Malay with her Malaysian friends. She started to learn Korean online after meeting Manshik. The couple speak mostly in English, but they occasionally mix in Korean or Chinese words. They were expecting a baby at the time of our interview.

Mark and Lydia
Mark is a Singaporean man who speaks English, as well as a bit of Hokkien and Mandarin. Lydia is Korean and moved to Singapore for work. She speaks Korean and English. The pair speak English together, as Mark does not know any Korean. The couple were expecting a baby at the time of our interview.

Mateo and Celine
Celine is a Korean woman who speaks Korean as her first language. Growing up, she lived in New Zealand for a period of time, so she speaks English too. She began studying Spanish when she was 15 and has now been speaking it for 20 years. She works as a Spanish teacher in Singapore. Mateo is a Spanish man who is working in Singapore. Before this, he worked in Korea for two and a half years. He speaks Spanish, and English as he learnt it in high school. He tried to learn Korean when he lived in Korea, but he did not progress past beginner level. Mateo and Celine met when Celine was travelling in Spain. Mateo then moved to Korea to be with her. After that, they moved to Singapore together. The couple speak a mix of Spanish and English in their daily lives.

Jack and Iola
Jack is an American man who grew up in the US and has lived in India, Malaysia, and Singapore for work as an adult. Iola is a Singaporean woman who speaks English as her first language, as well as some Cantonese, Hokkien, and Mandarin. The couple met in Malaysia and maintained a long-distance relationship between Malaysia and Singapore for a while. They now live in Singapore, where they speak English as their main language.

Alejandro and Jihye

Alejandro is a Singaporean man of Chinese heritage. Growing up, he spoke mainly English at home, as well as some Hokkien and Mandarin. Jihye is a Korean woman who speaks Korean as her first language. She also speaks English, as she lived in the Philippines for a few years as a child, where English is widespread. She moved to Singapore to work as a Korean language teacher. The couple speak English as their main language.

Charles and Reina

Charles is a Singaporean man who has Chinese, Indonesian, and Malaysian heritage. He speaks English, Mandarin, Malay, and some Hokkien. Reina was born in Singapore. Her father is Indian Singaporean and her mother is Japanese. Her parents met when they were studying in New Zealand. Eventually, they moved to Singapore. Reina learnt to speak Japanese from her mother, although her family mostly spoke English together. Charles and Reina speak English together.

Bob and Lark

Lark is Chinese Singaporean. She grew up in Singapore speaking English and Mandarin. She also speaks Cantonese at home with her family. She learnt Korean growing up. She met Bob through a friend, who brought them together because Lark could speak Korean. Bob was born and raised in Korea. His first language is Korean, but he also speaks English. His English was not at a very high level when he first moved to Singapore, but it has since improved. The pair speak in Korean 80% of the time, occasionally using English when needed.

Aimee and Sean

Aimee grew up in Britain and the US and has citizenship in both countries. She currently lives in Singapore. Her partner, Sean, is of Korean origin but has lived in the US for more than 20 years. Although she wants to learn Korean, her partner is highly proficient in English. This gives her little motivation to learn the Korean language. She did not know much about Korea before she met Sean. She said that her definition of 'comfort food' changed. Although they are from different countries, she said her childhood experience is very similar to Sean's.

Translanguaging: A Tool for Enabling Intercultural Couples

Translanguaging characterises the language and literacy practices of multilingual individuals, insofar as they not only go back and forth between two languages, but also flexibly and creatively interweave various linguistic features from two or more languages into their language and literacy practice (García & Li, 2014). Intercultural couples with multiple linguistic repertoires seamlessly travel around languages and create borderless languages of their own. These couples are always translating, always experimenting, and always learning, through dynamic multimodal interaction. However, they also know the differences between the languages, particularly their nuanced meanings and cultural norms. They translanguage creatively, using all the verbal and non-verbal resources available to them to create meaning. Flexibility and creativity are indeed at the heart of language practice, as we shall observe in this book. Through research with ICs and their family languages, we will show the innovative dimensions of their interactions that go beyond just a verbal exchange. Translanguaging is a linguistically enabling tool. It is a practice by which spouses make room for their partners, and particularly for immigrant spouses, when a couple is living in the home country of one spouse. Many immigrant spouses suffer isolation or loneliness. Translanguaging practices can help to ensure that couples can engage or re-engage in satisfying communication, and thus can flourish.

Translanguaging practices are something that couples need to navigate and explore throughout their lifetimes to find what suits their relationship best. They need to maximise their linguistic and cultural resources in an inclusive way, so as not to kill off one partner's language and culture for the sake of unity. In doing so, they optimise their differences, bringing about greater equality and celebrating diversity. If there is linguistic dominance and if the aim is to assimilate one partner into the other's culture completely, then tension and conflicts often arise. One-sided or unnegotiated differences are unsatisfying to both parties, thus leading to resentment. ICs face unique challenges because while some differences might seem personal, they can actually be the result of different cultures. Thus, the conflicts that ICs face involve the larger society too. This is why there is a strong need for the understanding and appreciation of each other's cultures. Picking just one spouse's culture and language will never be successful. Instead, ICs embark on a lifelong process of negotiation which is mediated through translanguaging. Translanguaging is an important social practice that enables intercultural couples to thrive. Without translanguaging, having one dominant language or culture will be disabling for the couple and ultimately their happiness.

Translanguaging is a dynamic meaning making process by which one employs diverse semiotic resources across the borders of language. Think of translanguaging as being like cooking. Even if two people are cooking the same dish, they will tailor-make the dish to suit their tastes. In intercultural couples, dishes often combine different cultural staples. For example, a fried egg can be eaten in many different ways across the globe. Some people eat them on toast. Some people add soy sauce, much to others' horror. Some add sriracha. If you are cooking for someone, and you know that they prefer their egg with soy sauce, then you would of course provide them with soy sauce, even if it is not your preference. You adapt to their needs to make them feel more comfortable, even if it is not the cultural norm in your country. Likewise, during festivals, ICs creatively choose which food to eat to suit the whole family. In the UK, it is traditional to eat turkey on Christmas Day, but in East Asia, it is traditional to eat dumplings. Thus, a British-East Asian couple might choose to have turkey and dumplings as their Christmas dinner. Festival food can be a source of tension, but it also provides the opportunity for innovation and coming together. Much like translanguaging, it is an enabling experience. This way of combining foods in a borderless and culture-blurring manner mimics how translanguaging works.

The fluid and innovative nature of translanguaging can capture and explain the complex linguistic and cultural experiences of multilingual families and how ICs with diverse backgrounds can make sense of their multilingual world. The term was originally coined in Welsh as *trawsieithu* by Cen Williams in the 1980s (Conteh, 2018, p. 445), before being translated into English as 'translanguaging' by Colin Baker, who introduced the term as a verb to capture the nature of the phenomenon as a process rather than a result. 'Translanguaging' was then developed further by other researchers. Baker (2011, p. 288) defined translanguaging as the process of 'making meaning, shaping experiences, gaining understanding and knowledge through the use of two languages'. Translanguaging goes beyond code-switching, as it shows a hybridity of language use that transcends the typical features of any single language involved.

Although many assume that translanguaging practices, such as fluidly switching and incorporating different languages into one's speech, are a transitional behaviour that children will eventually grow out of once they become more linguistically competent, translanguaging is far from transitional. Rather, it is a useful linguistic tool that forms part of everyday language for multilingual speakers and families throughout their lives. As Cenoz and Gorter (2021) demonstrate, translanguaging is a skill that aids the development of bilingualism. It is a unique, fluid bilingual process that can make multilingual speakers creative and efficient in their speech, while helping them build solidarity with other multilinguals through their shared linguistic experiences. The lexicons of multilingual families cannot be described in only one language, as they comprise a blend of words from languages tailor-made to each family. When a child says a word from another language in an English sentence, they have not made a mistake or failed in constructing a 'proper' English sentence. Rather, they have succeeded in conveying a nuanced meaning by fully applying their multilingual repertoire. The lens of translanguaging will allow us to interpret ICs and their family members' uses of non-English words as being creative, rather than erroneous. These behaviours are natural and pragmatically optimal. Translanguaging behaviours are not simply a steppingstone for proficiency in one language, but are in themselves a natural, productive language system. As Nakamura and Quay (2012) suggest, translanguaging is a complex interaction between the amount of input, language preference, child's personality, and how caregivers respond to language mixing. Often, one language alone is inadequate to efficiently convey nuanced meanings in many cases. Our lives and languages are now connected on a global scale. As the world becomes more and more virtually interconnected, the distinctions between nation state, ethnicity, and identity will become even more blurred. As a result, the practice of translanguaging will become more common than ever before—not only for a limited population but for everyone as virtual mobility soars. This book takes the framework of translanguaging to look at how ICs negotiate and navigate two or more languages. We focus on the cultural gaps between Asian and Western cultures, and how translanguaging can be used to create attitudinal and emotional meanings accordingly. By looking at these aspects through the lens of translanguaging, we will begin to see how translanguaging is an enriching and nurturing feature of ICs' lives.

STRUCTURE

This book outlines the problems that intercultural couples and their families face in the course of everyday communication, both amongst themselves and with others, and looks at how they can then be understood within the study of intercultural communication. Each chapter of this book explores a different issue in the lives of intercultural couples: language, emotion, wider family and friends, and culture. In these chapters, readers will find selected extracts from our interviews with ICs that are related to these topics. We highlight how interactions are negotiated both in the offline and online worlds, as technology currently is such an important part of our lives. We will see that intercultural couples face a multitude of challenges. What poses a challenge for one couple might pose no issue for another. This book by no means aims to generalise the experiences of ICs; instead, we aim to highlight the breadth of highs and lows that ICs face, and some of the issues that they have to navigate.

Despite the fact that verbal and non-verbal elements of language are intrinsically and inseparably linked, it is rare to see the non-verbal features of language acquisition closely examined alongside their verbal counterparts. How we say something is just as important, if not more so, as the words and grammar that we use. This is especially true for spouses who may not have perfect linguistic competence. To overcome any lack of linguistic competency, spouses will use gesture and pitch. Although these are useful tools, they require intercultural understanding too. For example, Menzies (2015) found that volume is used differently in different cultures. In British culture, an increase in volume commonly signals anger, whilst in India, it can be used to command attention. Menzies also found that Asians and Europeans speak at a quieter volume than North Americans on average. Thus, intercultural communication goes beyond words. Throughout the book, we will show the challenges that ICs face, and the dynamic, multifaceted processes of negotiation that they go through to make communication happen—both verbally and non-verbally.

In some chapters, there will be tip boxes with suggestions about how best to navigate some of the common issues faced by ICs. Although there is no one-size-fits-all approach, we hope that readers will be able to benefit from some of our suggestions, adapting them to suit their own unique needs.

The contents of the book can be summarised as follows.

Chapter 2, *Language Negotiation*, looks at the daily language practice choices that our ICs have made. It focuses on pragmatic language choices. We find that, broadly speaking, our couples can be divided into three categories: those who speak both spouses' first languages, those who speak only one of the spouse's first languages, and those who speak a third language, that is neither spouses' first language. These choices have their own benefits and difficulties. All of them involve some degree of translanguaging. This chapter will consider the importance of making an effort to learn your spouse's first language and the impact that speaking only one spouse's first language can have on an immigrant spouse.

Chapter 3, *Language of Emotion*, moves beyond the daily practicalities of language choice to consider how our couples express emotion through language. We consider the motivations behind ICs' translanguaging using the 3 Es Model proposed by Kiaer (2021). The model proposes that we make language choices according to three factors: efficiency, emotion, and expressivity. This chapter looks at how our couples switch between languages to show affection, express anger and frustration, and create humour. We highlight that translanguaging is not just a pragmatic tool that allows for efficient communication: crucially, it is an emotive resource that allows for greater expressivity and building solidarity between and beyond the boundaries of languages.

Chapter 4, *Language with Wider Family*, explores how ICs communicate with their in-laws, their children, and their friends. This book focuses mostly on Asian-Western couples. The chapter will highlight that familial expectations in the West and in Asia vary greatly. In Asian countries, parents-in-law expect to be treated with a high level of respect. In Western countries, parents-in-law are happy to have a friendly relationship with their children-in-law. We will see that most of our ICs cannot communicate fully with their parents-in-law due to language barriers, and so we look at how our ICs employ translanguaging to overcome linguistic and cultural differences. We also explore the language practices that our ICs employ with their children. Some spouses avoid teaching their children their first language so as not to confuse them, even though there is no scientific evidence that children will be confused by two or more languages. Elsewhere, many ICs speak both partners' first languages with their children, often from cultural motivation, rather than linguistic needs. Finally, we will look at the importance of friends and how speaking to friends in their first language can provide a reprieve for immigrant spouses and couples. This chapter highlights the extensive uses of translanguaging and its benefits in larger communities.

Chapter 5, *Language of Culture*, discusses the negotiations that ICs make to navigate their cultural differences. We consider a wide variety of activities and events that are linked to one's cultural background, including food, festivals, weddings, finance, household labour, and general ideology. Our ICs' responses highlight the importance of making an effort to understand and celebrate your spouse's festivals and food. Learning about each other's cultural traditions is a decisive act of care, as festivals and food hold so much meaning for our ICs. We also reflect on weddings and the decisions that our couples have made about having a wedding in either one or both of their cultures. We then look at how our couples manage practicalities such as finance and household labour in light of their different cultural backgrounds. We find that frequent conflict arises from differences in culture, as compared with the other topic areas discussed in earlier chapters. ICs always make language work for them by compromising and making pragmatic decisions. Culture is a more emotional issue for ICs and so it is important that they consider how to improve their understanding of their spouse's culture and the significance it has in their lives to avoid seeming uncaring.

References

Abela, A., Piscopo, S., & Vella, S. (2020). Understanding love relationships in a global context: Supporting couples across cultures. In *Couple relationships in a global context* (pp. 3–17). Springer. https://doi.org/10.1007/978-3-030-37712-0_1

Ahn, H. (2017). English as a discursive and social communication resource for contemporary S. Koreans. In C. Jenks & J. W. Lee (Eds.), *Korean Englishes in transnational contexts* (pp. 157–179). Palgrave Macmillan.

Amrith, S. S. (2014). Migration and health in southeast Asian history. *The Lancet (British edition), 384*(9954), 1569–1570.

Baker, C. (2011). *The foundations of Bilingual Education and Bilingualism*. Bristol, UK: Multilingual Matters.

Baxter, L. A. (1987). Symbols of relationship identity in relationship cultures. *Journal of Social & Personal Relationships, 4*(3), 261–280.

Baxter, L. A. (2004). A tale of two voices: Relational dialectics theory. *Journal of Family Communication, 4*(3/4), 181–192.

Baxter, L. A., & Montgomery, B. M. (1996). *Relating: Dialogues and dialectics*. Guilford Press.

Berg-Cross, L. (2001). *Couples therapy*. Hawthorne.

Bhugun, D. (2017). Intercultural parenting in Australia. *The Family Journal, 25*(2), 187–195. https://doi.org/10.1177/1066480717697688

Bhugun, D. (2019). *Intercultural parenting and relationships: Challenges and rewards* (1st ed.). Springer International Publishing. https://doi.org/10.1007/978-3-030-14060-1

Brahic, B. (2013). The politics of bi-nationality in couple relationships: A case study of European bi-national couples in Manchester. *Journal of Comparative Family Studies, 44*(6), 699–714. https://doi.org/10.3138/jcfs.44.6.699

Bratter, J. L., & King, R. B. (2008). "But will it last?": Marital instability among interracial and same-race couples. *Family Relations, 57*(2), 160–171.

Brummett, E. A., & Steuber, K. R. (2015). To reveal or conceal?: Privacy management processes among interracial romantic partners. *Western Journal of Communication, 79*(1), 22–44.

Bustamante, R. M., Nelson, J. A., Henriksen, R. C., & Monakes, S. (2011). Intercultural couples: Coping with culture-related stressors. *The Family Journal, 19*(2), 154–164. https://doi.org/10.1177/1066480711399723

Bystydzienski, J. M. (2011). *Intercultural couples: Crossing boundaries, negotiating difference*. New York University Press.

Canagarajah, S. (2011). Translanguaging in the classroom: Emerging issues for research and pedagogy. *Applied Linguistics Review, 2*(1), 1–28.

Canagarajah, A. S. (2013). *Translingual practice global Englishes and cosmopolitan relations*. Routledge.

Canagarajah, S., & Dovchin, S. (2019). The everyday politics of translingualism as a resistant practice. *International Journal of Multilingualism, 16*(2), 127–144.

Cenoz, J., & Gorter, D. (2021). *Pedagogical translanguaging*. Cambridge University Press.

Cerchiaro, F. (2017). 'In the name of the children': Mixed couples' parenting analysed through their naming practices. *Identities, 26*(1), 51–68. https://doi.org/10.1080/1070289x.2017.1353314

Chi, Y.-F. (2014). *Multilingual couples' disagreement: Taiwanese partners and their foreign spouses*. University of London.

Constable, N. (2003). *Romance on a global stage: Pen pals, virtual ethnography, and "mail order" marriages*. University of California Press. http://www.jstor.org/stable/10.1525/j.ctt1pnr50

Constable, N. (Ed.). (2005). *Cross-border marriages: Gender and mobility in transnational Asia*. University of Pennsylvania Press. http://www.jstor.org/stable/j.ctt3fhv66

Conteh, J. (2018). Translanguaging. *ELT Journal, 72*(4), 445–447.

Coupland, N., Wiemann, J. M., & Giles, H. (1991). Talk as "problem" and communication as "miscommunication": An integrative analysis. In N. Coupland, J. M. Wiemann, & H. Giles (Eds.), *"Miscommunication" and problematic talk* (pp. 1–17). SAGE Publication.

Dervin, F. (2013). Do intercultural couples "see culture everywhere"? *Civilisations,* 62, 131–148. https://doi.org/10.4000/civilisations.3352

Dewaele, J.-M. (2013). *Emotions in multiple languages.* Palgrave Macmillan.

Dewaele, J.-M. (2015). From obscure echo to language of the heart: Multilinguals' language choices for (emotional) inner speech. *Journal of Pragmatics, 87,* 1–17. https://doi.org/10.1016/j.pragma.2015.06.014

Dewaele, J.-M. (2016). Thirty shades of offensiveness: L1 and LX English users' understanding, perception and self-reported use of negative emotion-laden words. *Journal of Pragmatics, 94,* 112–127. https://doi.org/10.1016/j.pragma.2016.01.009

Dewaele, J.-M. (2018a). Pragmatic challenges in the communication of emotions in intercultural couples. *Intercultural Pragmatics, 15*(1), 29–55. https://doi.org/10.1515/ip-2017-0029

Dewaele, J.-M. (2018b). Why the dichotomy 'L1 versus LX user' is better than 'native versus non-native speaker'. *Applied Linguistics, 39*(2), 236–240.

Dewaele, J.-M., & Salomidou, L. (2017). Loving a partner in a foreign language. *Journal of Pragmatics, 108,* 116–130. https://doi.org/10.1016/j.pragma.2016.12.009

Epp, A. M., Schau, H. J., & Price, L. L. (2014). The role of brands and mediating technologies in assembling long-distance family practices. *Journal of Marketing, 78*(3), 81–101.

Falicov, C. J. (1995). Cross-cultural marriages. In *Clinical handbook of couple therapy* (pp. 231–246). Guilford.

Fu, X., & Heaton, T. B. (2000). Status exchange in intermarriage among Hawaiians, Japanese, Filipinos and Caucasians in Hawaii: 1983–1994. *Journal of Comparative Family Studies, 31*(1), 45–61. https://doi.org/10.3138/jcfs.31.1.45

García, O., & Leiva, C. (2014). Theorising and enacting translanguaging for social justice. In A. Blackledge & A. Creese (Eds.), *Heteroglossia as practice and pedagogy* (pp. 199–216). Springer.

García, O., & Li, W. (2014). *Translanguaging: Language, bilingualism and education.* Palgrave Macmillan. http://ezlibproxy1.ntu.edu.sg/login?url=http://search.ebscohost.com/login.aspx?direct=true&db=cat00103a&AN=ntu.a1295037&site=eds-live&scope=site

Gibbons, J. (1987). *Code-mixing and code choice: A Hong Kong case study.* Multilingual Matters.

Gumperz, J. C. (1982). *Discourse strategies.* Cambridge University Press.

Gumperz, J. J., & Gumperz, J. C. (1981). Ethnic differences in communicative style. In C. Ferguson & S. Heath (Eds.), *Language in the USA* (pp. 430–445). Cambridge University Press.

Hirschmann, R. (2021). *Estimated number of Asian immigrants in Singapore in 2020, by country of origin,* Statista. Available at: https://www.statista.com/

statistics/692951/asian-immigrant-stock-of-singapore-by-country-of-origin/. Accessed November 17, 2022.

Hirschmann, R. (2022). *Number of immigrants in Singapore from 2005 to 2020, Statista*. Available at: https://www.statista.com/statistics/698035/singapore-number-of-immigrants/. Accessed November 17, 2022.

Iwakabe, S. (2019). Working through shame with an intercultural couple in Japan: Transforming negative emotional interactions and expanding positive emotional resources. *Journal of Clinical Psychology, 75*(11), 2060–2071. https://doi.org/10.1002/jclp.22864

Kalmijn, M. (1998). Intermarriage and homogamy: Causes, patterns, trends. *Annual Review of Sociology, 24*, 395–421.

Kashyap, L. (2020). Changing couple relationships in India. In *Couple relationships in a global context* (pp. 71–83). Springer. https://doi.org/10.1007/978-3-030-37712-0_5

Kiaer, J. (2021). *Pragmatic particles: Findings from Asian languages*. Bloomsbury. (Bloomsbury studies in theoretical linguistics).

Kiaer, J., Kim, L., Hua, Z., & Wei, L. (2022). Tomorrow? Jayaji! (자야지) Translation as translanguaging in interviews with the Director of Parasite. *Translation and Translanguaging in Multilingual Contexts, 8*(3), 260–284.

Kim, E. (2006). Reasons and motivations for code-mixing and code-switching. *EFL, 4*(Spring 2006), 43–61.

Kline, S. L., Horton, B., & Zhang, S. (2008). Communicating love: Comparisons between American and east Asian university students. *International Journal of Intercultural Relations, 32*(3), 200–214. https://doi.org/10.1016/j.ijintrel.2008.01.006

Kroeber, A. L., & Kluckhohn, C. (1963). *Culture: A critical review of concepts and definitions* (1st Vintage ed.). Vintage Books.

Kull, A. (2018). *Perceived communication of emotion in intercultural Estonian-Australian couples*. The University of Queensland.

Lawton, B., Foeman, A., & Braz, M. (2013). Interracial couples' conflict styles on educational issues. *Journal of Intercultural Communication Research, 42*(1), 35–53. https://doi.org/10.1080/17475759.2012.711766

Le Gall, J., & Meintel, D. (2015). Cultural and identity transmission in mixed couples in Quebec, Canada. *The Annals of the American Academy of Political and Social Science, 662*(1), 112–128. https://doi.org/10.1177/0002716215602705

Lee, J. (2005). Korean-English bilinguals (KEB) vs. English monolinguals (EM): Language and international marriage partnership. In *The 4th International Symposium on Bilingualism*.

Lee, J. W. (2022). Translanguaging research methodologies. *Research Methods in Applied Linguistics, 1*(1), 100004.

Lee, J., & Bean, F. D. (2004). America's changing color lines: Immigration, race/ethnicity, and multiracial identification. *Annual Review of Sociology*, 30, 221–242.

Lee, J. W., & Canagarajah, S. (2021). Translingualism and world Englishes. *Bloomsbury World Englishes Volume 1: Paradigms*, 1, 99.

Leeds-Hurwitz, W. (2009). Ambiguity as a solution to the "problem" of intercultural weddings. In T. Karis & K. Killian (Eds.), *Intercultural couples: Exploring diversity in intimate relationships* (pp. 167–187). Routledge.

Li, W. (2011). Moment analysis and translanguaging space: Discursive construction of identities by multilingual Chinese youth in Britain. *Journal of Pragmatics*, 43(5), 1222–1235.

Li, W. (2018). Translanguaging as a practical theory of language. *Applied Linguistics*, 39(1), 9–30. https://doi.org/10.1093/applin/amx039

Mazzaferro, G. (2018). Language maintenance and shift within new linguistic minorities in Italy: A translanguaging perspective. In G. Mazzaferro (Ed.), *Translanguaging as everyday practice* (pp. 87-106). Springer International Publishing. https://doi.org/10.1007/978-3-319-94851-5_6

Menzies, F. (2015). *Paralanguage across cultures, include-empower.com*. Available at: https://culturepulsconsulting.com/2015/04/16/paralanguage-across-cultures/. Accessed November 17, 2022.

Milroy, L., & Gordon, M. J. (2003). *Sociolinguistics: Method and interpretation*. Blackwell.

Molina, B., Estrada, D., & Burnett, J. A. (2004). Cultural communities: Challenges and opportunities in the creation of "happily ever after" stories of intercultural couplehood. *The Family Journal*, 12(2), 139–147. https://doi.org/10.1177/1066480703261962

Moyer, M. G. (1997). One speaker, two languages: Cross-disciplinary perspectives on code-switching. *Journal of Linguistic Anthropology*, 7(2), 237–239. https://doi.org/10.1525/jlin.1997.7.2.237

Muysken, P. (2000). *Bilingual speech. A typology of code-switching*. Cambridge University Press.

Myers-Scotton, C. (1993). *Duelling languages: Grammatical structure in codeswitching*. Oxford University Press.

Naldic. (n.d.). *NALDIC | EAL Statistics | EAL Achievement*. https://www.naldic.org.uk/research-and-information/eal-statistics/ealachievement/

Nakamura, J., & Quay, S. (2012). The impact of caregivers' interrogative styles in English and Japanese on early bilingual development. *International Journal of Bilingual Education and Bilingualism*, 15(4), 417–434.

Pietikäinen, K. S. (2016). Misunderstandings and ensuring understanding in private ELF talk. *Applied Linguistics*, 39(2), 188–212. https://doi.org/10.1093/applin/amw005

Piller, I. (2002). *Bilingual couples talk: The discursive construction of hybridity*. John Benjamins.
Piller, I. (2007). Cross-cultural communication in intimate relationships. In H. Kotthoff & H. Spencer-Oatey (Eds.), *Intercultural communication* (pp. 341–359). Mouton de Gruyter.
Piller, I. (2009). I always wanted to marry a cowboy: Bilingual couples, language, and desire. In T. Karis & K. Killian (Eds.), *Intercultural couples: Exploring diversity in intimate relationships* (pp. 53–70). Taylor & Francis.
Piller, I. (2017). *Intercultural communication: A critical introduction* (2nd ed.). Edinburgh University Press.
Quah, S. R. (2003). Ethnicity and parenting styles among Singapore families. *Marriage and Family Review, 35*(3), 63–83.
Rogan, D., Piacentini, M., & Hopkinson, G. (2018). Intercultural household food tensions: A relational dialectics analysis. *European Journal of Marketing, 52*(12), 2289–2311. https://doi.org/10.1108/ejm-10-2017-0778
Rosenblatt, P. C. (2011). A systems theory analysis of intercultural couple relationships. In *Intercultural couples* (pp. 24–41). Routledge.
Scollon, R., & Scollon, S. W. (2001). Discourse and intercultural communication. In D. Schiff & H. Hamilton (Eds.), *The handbook of discourse analysis* (pp. 538–547). Blackwell Wiley.
Scollon, R., Scollon, S. W., & Jones, R. H. (2012). *Intercultural communication: A discourse approach*. John Wiley & Sons, Incorporated. http://ebookcentral.proquest.com/lib/unimelb/detail.action?docID=822409
Seshadri, G., & Knudson-Martin, C. (2013). How couples manage interracial and intercultural differences: Implications for clinical practice. *Journal of Marital and Family Therapy, 39*(1), 43–58. https://doi.org/10.1111/j.1752-0606.2011.00262.x
Shenhav, S., Campos, B., & Goldberg, W. A. (2016). Dating out is intercultural. *Journal of Social and Personal Relationships, 34*(3), 397–422. https://doi.org/10.1177/0265407516640387
Skowroński, D., Ying Cherie, T. S., Fernandez, T. M., Fong Tay Danx, D., Ho Wen Wan, M., & Waszyńska, K. (2014). Introductory analysis of factors affecting intercultural couples in the context of Singapore. *Studia Edukacyjne, 30*, 263–268. https://doi.org/10.14746/se.2014.30.15
Stępkowska, A. (2021). Identity in the bilingual couple: Attitudes to language and culture. *Open Linguistics, 7*(1), 223–234. https://doi.org/10.1515/opli-2021-0020
Takigawa, Y. (2010). *Language expertise as a source of dispute in bilingual couple talk*. Temple University. http://hdl.handle.net/20.500.12613/2502
Tan, C. L.-L. (2016). *Sarong party girls*. HarperCollins.
Tannen, D. (1986). *That's not what I meant!* Ballantine Books.

Taweekuakulkit, N. (2005). *Thai-north American intercultural marriage in the United States: A qualitative study of conflict from Thai wives' perspectives*. Wayne State University.

Tay, M. W. J. (1989). Code switching and code mixing as a communicative strategy in multilingual discourse. *World Englishes, 8*(3), 407–417. https://doi.org/10.1111/j.1467-971X.1989.tb00678.x

Tien, N. C. (2013). *Communication and relationships of intercultural/multilingual couples: Cultural and language differences*. University of Colorado.

UK Department for Education. (June 9, 2022). Percentage of pupils whose first language is known or believed to be other than English in England from 2015/16 to 2021/22 [Graph]. In *Statista*. Retrieved June 21, 2023, from https://www.statista.com/statistics/330782/england-english-additional-language-primary-pupils/

Zhang, Y., & Van Hook, J. (2009). Marital dissolution among interracial couples. *Journal of Marriage and Family, 71*(1), 95–107.

Zhu, H, Li., W., & Lyons, A. (2017). Polish shop(ping) as translanguaging space. *Social Semiotics, 27*(4), 411–433. https://doi.org/10.1080/10350330.2017.1334390

Zhu, H. (2019). *Exploring intercultural communication: Language in action*. Routledge.

CHAPTER 2

Language Negotiation

Abstract Language matters to ICs. Successful communication is the key to a happy relationship. The more diverse the linguistic and cultural repertoire of a couple, the more complex the linguistic negotiation will be. Complex linguistic negotiation is a growing issue as global mobility is increasing. Many couples do not choose just one of their languages to be the main language of their communication; instead they use multiple languages seamlessly to mediate the two, three, four, or more languages that they have between them. At times, this process can be frustrating, as one or both partners may not be able to express themselves fully in the chosen main language. Inevitably, the couple choose a dominant language for the sake of practicality, but it is important that the process of finding the dominant language involves healthy discussion and debate. One should also know that the dominant language is always negotiable. Choosing the dominant language is not about shutting down the other language(s) in the relationship completely. Instead, it is about finding the combination that works best for the couple and family. The dominant language, for example, might change according to the location where a couple resides. In this respect, we recommend that translanguaging practices form a part of intercultural couples' daily communication. These practices enable the couple's linguistic diversity. This is particularly beneficial to immigrant spouses, who are linguistically and culturally vulnerable to the disabling of their heritage and background.

Language matters to ICs. Successful communication is the key to a happy relationship. The more diverse the linguistic and cultural repertoire of a couple, the more complex the linguistic negotiation will be. Complex linguistic negotiation is a growing issue as global mobility is increasing. Many couples do not choose just one of their languages to be the main language of their communication; instead they use multiple languages seamlessly to mediate the two, three, four, or more languages that they have between them. At times, this process can be frustrating, as one or both partners may not be able to express themselves fully in the chosen main language. Inevitably, the couple choose a dominant language for the sake of practicality, but it is important that the process of finding the dominant language involves healthy discussion and debate. One should also know that the dominant language is always negotiable. Choosing the dominant language is not about shutting down the other language(s) in the relationship completely. Instead, it is about finding the combination that works best for the couple and family. The dominant language, for example, might change according to the location where a couple resides. In this respect, we recommend that translanguaging practices form a part of intercultural couples' daily communication. These practices enable the couple's linguistic diversity. This is particularly beneficial to immigrant spouses, who are linguistically and culturally vulnerable to the disabling of their heritage and background.

Translanguaging practices promote greater inclusivity, but there is no simple formula that all couples can follow. Every couple has to embark on their own process of negotiation. We will see examples of this in Chap. 5. What we find is that couples compartmentalise their dominant language based on differing needs. In doing so, they make their communication both efficient and more emotionally enriched. This highlights that imposing one language or judging or criticising your spouse's language only creates a negative impact. It is important to be open towards each other and to mutually make the effort to learn at least some of each other's languages. With patience and care, couples can achieve enriched and emotionally satisfying communication.

Learning Together: He Had to Force himself to Speak Chinese

The couples that we interviewed can be broadly divided into three categories: (1) those who predominantly speak in neither of the couple's first languages, (2) those who mainly speak in just one of the couple's first languages, and (3) those who mix both their L1s closer to a 50/50 split. None of these three communication choices are superior to the other, although each one poses different challenges. Couples decide how to communicate constantly and dynamically because each situation brings something new. For example, couples may change which language they predominantly use together depending on where they are living. It is a choice that first and foremost affects the couple, and then also affects family and close friends. Below, Jane describes how the language that she and Tony speak together has changed over time:

> Jane: Yeah actually at the beginning, we spoke English all the time, because he was only in China for one year, so I assumed his Chinese was not good enough. Whenever he speaks Chinese, it sounded so correct and so proper, so I thought, "Wow he's got talent in terms of language", so I started speaking a little bit of Chinese to him. I'm not very patient, but in terms of speaking Chinese to him, I was super patient. If he couldn't get it, I would explain it to him, and then I also told him that, "Okay, since you live in China, if you don't speak Chinese with me, you have no chance to learn Chinese unless you go to a proper school". So I said "Let's speak Chinese" and he agreed at the beginning, but he felt it was so challenging. He couldn't speak in a complete sentence, he said he was so frustrated and then he said "Okay let's switch back to English." I agreed, but the funny thing was whenever we switched back to English, I had no reaction. When he told me stories, I would reply like "mmm mmm". But whenever he switched back to Chinese, I was super patient and I listened to him and I reacted to him, so he had to force himself to speak Chinese. so now, our language is actually Chinese.

Jane's first language is Korean, although she grew up in Northern China, whilst Tony's first language is English. Chinese became the couple's mutual language through negotiation, both explicitly and implicitly. During this process, which took around three months, there was both cooperation and competition between them, with the former being the dominant trend. At the initial stages, Chinese was not taken as the couple's mutual language; as for many others, English served as the medium of cross-cultural communication. The transition started with Tony's active use of certain Chinese words in his speech, which encouraged Jane to believe that they could communicate in Chinese someday. Though Jane regarded herself as an impatient person on other occasions, she showed great patience in explaining Chinese to Tony. Later, when Tony felt frustrated by the difficulty of Chinese language learning and proposed to switch back to English, Jane didn't say no. Jane mentions that she had lacklustre reactions to Tony speaking in English, but whether this was deliberate or not is unclear. As we will see in Chap. 3, languages are linked to emotion, and English might not be a highly emotive or impactful language for Jane. Whether deliberate or not, Tony was motivated to switch back to Chinese. Tony's active use of Chinese words from the very beginning, the efforts he put into speaking Chinese, and his compromise of switching back to Chinese in the end were all signs of him making an effort. Combined with Jane's help and patience, Jane and Tony negotiated their language from being the expected English to Mandarin, which is neither partner's first language.

Jane was particularly keen that Tony learn Mandarin, despite the fact that she would not consider it her first language. Jane mentioned that she did not speak Mandarin comfortably until after she went to university and started working. She said, 'Whenever I speak Chinese people know that I'm not Chinese Chinese', highlighting that her identity is tied more to her Korean heritage than her geographical location in China. Thus, her motivation to help Tony learn Mandarin was likely also a compromise on her part. Both Tony and Jane were working in China at the time in an English- and Mandarin-speaking environment, so Tony learning Mandarin would have seemed a more viable option than him learning Korean, a language he has had little exposure to. For Jane, it was about balancing their mutual languages. She stated, 'I know English better than your Chinese, so actually you should learn Chinese'. Tony's reasoning is a little different:

> Tony: Out of the desire on my part to improve my Chinese and be a more confident user and kind of prove to myself and people around me that I could use the language, so I spoke more to her. And I guess with before we got together with colleagues and things like that in Chinese as much as I possibly could, but when we first got together, we did speak English because I didn't have a very good grasp of Chinese language. After maybe six months or so together, we switched to Chinese for the reasons that I have mentioned. But it all, it was almost a case of just switching one day and, and never going back.

Learning Mandarin was almost a point of pride, as he did not want to be living in China without being able to speak Mandarin. Tony describes the couple's main language moving from English to Mandarin as being fluid and simple: 'it was almost a case of just switching one day and, and never going back'.

Jane, however, remembers the difficulties:

> Interviewer: Do you think your husband felt disadvantaged because you chose to speak Mandarin together?
>
> Jane: At the beginning, yes. I felt so frustrated that I had to translate both English and Chinese in my head. He also wanted to make sure the sentence was correct. And sometimes he didn't know the word, so he said, "I cannot express myself properly". I said, "Okay, in that case you can say it in English, and I can translate it back to you". He tried a little bit, but mixing English and Chinese meant he struggled even more. I said, "Okay in that case you speak completely in English, I will translate that situation in Chinese to you." It's more like teaching.

Tony felt he was unable to express himself satisfactorily in Mandarin at the beginning of their relationship. Jane showed great patience in teaching and encouraging Tony and also giving him room to use English when needed. This open attitude towards translanguaging in their communication played an important role in Tony's Chinese learning as well as in their long-term relationship. Once the couple started speaking Chinese with each other, they never went back to speaking in English. The fact that Tony describes this process as 'switching one day and, and never going back' shows how naturally their translanguaging practice occurs in their daily communication.

Translanguaging: Because It's Showing Respect to his Culture and Where he Comes from

Some of our couples reported using a mixture of both of their first languages. In other words, they use translanguaging regularly to improve their communication. Couples who heavily employ translanguaging often emphasise that they do this to make their communication fair. Below, Evelyn describes how she and her partner Sanghoon use a mix of their first languages, Korean and English:

> Evelyn: I learnt Korean for I think about 10 years and then I stopped. So, when I converse with my husband, it's a mixture of English and Korean.

When it is too difficult or when I'm feeling tired, then it will be mainly in English.

Interviewer: When do you use Korean most?

Evelyn: I think food is a common one. Things like waking up and going to sleep or going out or coming back home, the simple greetings.

Interviewer: Why do you use Korean in those situations?

Evelyn: I think it's a bit of a habit. Because, from the start of the relationship, we already mixed languages, I wanted to try and speak more Korean. I tried to speak as much Korean as I could with him back then, and I would say simple things, so I think kind of build up a habit that has lasted until today.

Interviewer: You guys have been together for seven years, has the use of language changed over the course of time you've been together?

Evelyn: It's about the same. I feel that it might be a bit closer to be closer to English maybe because after all English is not his main language, and he only picked it up a bit later so sometimes. I think speaking in Korean sort of, I can feel a bit more sincerity and closeness to him. I met him because I wanted to find a language exchange friend so I wanted to practice more of my Korean back then, but then when we met, we were happily chatting and then we realized that oh, we can really click, and we somehow connected. At that time, when I spoke to him in English, he would speak back in English. But for now, I think things have changed a bit for now like, if I speak in English and for him if he finds it a bit more convenient to just speak in Korean, he would speak back to me in Korean. He knows how much I can understand, so he would just speak back in Korean.

Interviewer: You know, do you feel it's important for you to speak your partner's language?

Evelyn: Yes.

Interviewer: Why is it important?

Evelyn: Because it's showing respect to his culture and where he comes from. And also, in a way, I feel it connects the couple stronger, than just to speak in a language that only one is speaking.

Interviewer: What about growing up with two languages, English and Chinese, do you think it's important for your partner to speak Chinese?

Evelyn: No. Because I don't think it's important because he can speak English, but if he doesn't speak English and let's say it's only purely in Korean today, I might feel like there is a need for him to at least pick up one of the languages to learn a bit la yeah. Either English or Chinese.

Similarly to Jane and Tony, Evelyn and Sanghoon spoke more English at the start of their relationship. They met online as language buddies, so their intention was always to share their languages and learn from each other. Evelyn notes that Sanghoon began to speak more Korean with her when he was sure that she would understand. Evelyn believes that learning each other's languages is an important way to acknowledge each other's cultures and backgrounds. Evelyn spoke Chinese and English at home growing up, so if Sanghoon had not have been able to speak English originally, she would have hoped that he would have learnt one of her first languages.

Having been together for seven years, the couple now mix Korean and English in their daily lives. In Evelyn's eyes, they often use Korean to talk about simple everyday things, like food and plans for the day. In Sanghoon's mind, they often use Korean to talk about Korean cultural productions:

> Interviewer: Which situations do you speak Korean in?
> Sanghoon: For example, if we're talking about Korean dramas, or anything to do with Korea. We usually use a lot of Korean words to discuss these topics, so naturally we speak Korean.

It is interesting to see which topics spring to our interviewees' minds first. Evelyn remembers making a lot of effort to speak Korean at the start of her relationship, and so her memory of speaking Korean relates to everyday activities. In comparison, Sanghoon remembers their discussions about Korea and Korean cultural products the most. He perhaps feels that it is easier or even necessary to use Korean words to discuss these topics properly, rather than English words that do not hold the same significance to him. Overall, their differing responses highlight how translanguaging and using both languages is the most dynamic method of communication for ICs. It can adapt to all sorts of situations and topics of conversation.

Translanguaging: We Sometimes Text in Norwegian

ICs are often international by nature, as well as being intercultural. They might live in neither person's home country, and they might move from country to country for work. In doing so, they end up learning bits and pieces of multiple languages. Wherever they go, they carry these languages with them, using them to create various attitudinal meanings. One of our couples, Marcus and Erika, have lived in Norway and Singapore together, whilst Erika lived in France before they met. Marcus speaks English as a first language and Erika speaks Slovak. They mix English, Norwegian, Slovak, and French together when they speak:

Erika: We will mostly speak in English, from the start, but maybe in those initial years we sometimes texted in Norwegian. Then, it was mostly just English, but I think our English was becoming more and more elaborate, because at the time my English was not so good, it was more like a "Frenchified" English. If I didn't understand something I would ask him, I asked him to explain, so I think now my English more just more flawless yeah. At that time, he was also trying to learn Slovak, so I will explain to him, but now, because we can't travel, he doesn't use it too much. Yeah actually yeah it's becoming more monolingual, but then he actually he wants Harry (their son) to learn Slovak and he is actually even more insistent than me I think. Last time, he was teaching him counting, so I just wrote everything down how we write it. Because it's like it's a bit different a lot of accents and different signs, so pronunciation is bit different and Marcus was really insisting that Harry properly recognize the words counting one to 10 yeah. So for him it is quite important that he speaks Slovak.

Interviewer: Can he speak French?

Erika: Yes, yes, I mean a bit. He learned French, he can still speak some French. Then when we were in Norway, we would sometimes speak in Norwegian. And yeah, but I think these days, mostly in English. Sometimes he would say some stuff in Slovak, like a few expressions like whenever outside, he'll say, "come" in Slovak. I think he likes that it gives him some kind of privacy, so that people around don't really understand. He doesn't try longer sentences in Slovak, I mean it's very nice of him, he learned on his own so he could speak to my family and there was a point when he was quite good in Slovak.

English naturally became Erika and Marcus's main mutual language because it had the greatest potential to be the lingua franca between the couple, despite both being able to speak other languages. At the initial stage, it was Marcus who spoke better English and helped Erika to improve her English language skills, while at the same time, Marcus also started learning Slovak and asked help from Erika. The interaction about language learning and use between the couple suggests an inclusive attitude towards different languages and cultures. Moreover, their active engagement with each other's first language indicates a spirit of mutual respect and equality.

The fact that they use English as their main language is actually advantageous in Erika's eyes, despite the fact that it is not her first language:

Interviewer: Because English is Marcus's first language and English is like your third or fourth language, do you sometimes feel advantaged or disadvantaged that your mutual language is English?

Erika: No, I find English quite convenient. I can't imagine living with someone who speaks Slovak, because it would be so boring, your native language. I find that English is a good choice because it's very economic and analytical. I find it's good for a relationship to have English as the main language, because you know, it saves time and gets straight to the point where, whereas in French it is, like, long sentences and you build up first and before you actually get to the main point. So when I went to Norway, my Norwegian professor he would be like, "Okay, Erika I know you you're studying in France, but you must use shorter sentences", because my sentences will be like three lines, but he was like, "No, no, you be like Viking, you just go straight to the point, say what you want to say, like, subject verb object done." Their sentences are like five words, so I find English somewhere in between, it's quite good, yeah. If we use Slovak, I think it's quite similar to English but it's the speed is faster, so that's one of my problems that both Harry and Marcus say: "When I speak Slovak I speak too fast." Harry has sometimes difficulties to catch, so I really have to talk like a teacher, pronounce articulate, whereas in English, I think that the intonation is such that you emphasise naturally, but if you speak in Slovak it's like a monotonous melody, so I think English is a good choice for couples.

Erika is very positive about taking her partner's first language as their mutual language. She evaluates their language choice from the perspective of efficiency, instead of relating language to one's power or status in a family. She also does not mind that they have settled in Singapore, which is Marcus's home country, despite her mother's concerns.

Erika: My mom would say that she thinks that for intercultural couples, it's better if they settle in a neutral country, so nobody's home country. Actually my mom is a bit special because she has a lot of theories about life, but some of them are conspiracy theories and everything. In her eyes, if it's not a third country, there will always be someone who will be at a disadvantage. So if there is a conflict, at the end of the day, you know, their people will protect their people. But it's not the case, so I find it is great, because we appreciate it like now with Harry, it's a great help. Actually the best way is really to settle down in someone's country unless you have other help right? Because then Harry can go and visit his grandparents and so on.

Erika is positive about residing in her partner's home country. She can see a lot of benefits in doing so and shows no resistance to this choice, despite her mother's concern that the spouse who lives in their partner's home country will be disadvantaged. However, Erika doesn't feel disadvantaged living in her partner's society. It is nice that her parents-in-law will look after their son, Harry, when they need it. She alludes that this saves the couple money. Erika's positive attitude towards speaking English also likely helps her to enjoy living in Singapore. She does not appear to feel disadvantaged linguistically or culturally. Erika and Marcus have thus successfully negotiated their language practice to satisfy both members of the couple, even the immigrant spouse. This was a relatively rare find amongst our interviewees.

Making Do with One Language: I Think he Can, but he Prefers Not to

Many of our couples communicate using just one of their first languages. This can be efficient, but it is often unsatisfactory for one member of the couple. Charlie and John speak together in Korean, which is John's first language. Charlie's first language is English, but John's English proficiency is quite low. The pair live in Singapore, but mostly speak in Korean together:

> Interviewer: Why don't you speak to him in English?
> Charlie: I do speak to him in English like when I am frustrated, I will also use English and then there are sometimes where I try to explain something to him. He has been learning English on his own for quite a while already, but he says in Singapore, the accent is different from what he used to learn, he is very used to US American English so when, like in Singapore, it's all a mix, it sounds different the English and there's a lot of local slang which he might not understand as well. When I speak to him, he does understand, but I have to explain slowly, or sometimes I speak too fast. Then he says, can you speak slower, then I am very impatient.
> Interviewer: I think you guys speak Korean to each other, because his English is not as good as your Korean.
> Charlie: Eh, but actually my Korean is not that good also, as sometimes I explain something in Korean that he actually says, "I don't get you". I just use very basic words. He still quite shy to speak English like yesterday, I asked him to order something, just a very simple thing like ordering food. Then he will say "Oh no you do instead". I think he can, I think but he

prefers not to. I don't know why and also I think he feels like he doesn't really have a lot of friends here.

Charlie only speaks to John in English when she is trying to explain something she can't explain in Korean. She finds it very frustrating and so does he. John has actually studied a lot of English but it was American English and with an American accent, so he finds it hard to understand the non-American accents that he hears in cosmopolitan Singapore. Charlie thus tries to use her Korean, as she sees that English is inefficient. However, John does not always understand what she is trying to say. John seems to have developed a complex about speaking English. John moved to Singapore, quitting his job in Korea, after meeting Charlie online. Prior to this, he had never lived outside of Korea. He seems to have found it hard to adapt to life in Singapore. He shows signs of Foreign Language Anxiety (FLA) because he lacks the confidence to use his English to order food. Charlie also notes that he has made very few friends in Singapore. Charlie tries to be accommodating of this, by using her Korean, but the communication is not always satisfactory for her. Charlie's response implies that she is feeling the burden of making up for her spouse's lack of language proficiency. This is one of the couples that have not managed to make their language practice completely optimal. Both appear to feel that their communication is lacking, so more effort is needed on both parts to improve their language proficiency.

Living for Such a Long Time with me and he Is Not Able to Speak Chinese: It's Really Bad

Another of our couples revealed a similar problem of language imbalance. Yiyi speaks Mandarin as her first language, and her husband Alonso's first language is Italian. Yiyi has learnt some Italian over the course of their relationship, and she is able to maintain a relationship with her mother-in-law using it. Alonso, in comparison, does not know much Mandarin at all. The couple mainly communicate in English, but Yiyi still notices the imbalance in their language proficiencies:

> Interviewer: Do you think it's important for him to speak Chinese?
> Yiyi: Yeah, it should be important, living for such a long time with me and he is not able to speak Chinese, it's really bad, too bad.
> Interviewer: Why do you think it's very important?

Yiyi: Um to communicate, it's my mother tongue, and so we can communicate better if he speaks a bit more Chinese. Every time we went out, we would have nothing to do, so I started to repeat a Chinese poem. Only 18 characters. So the first assignment is not even 5 characters, but yeah, he doesn't remember. It's funny and funny and I also talk to him in a way in my dialect, so it's funny. He don't understand, it's funny too.

Yiyi believes that Alonso should put in more effort to learn Mandarin, as he is married to someone who speaks Mandarin. She wants them to be able to communicate more effectively, and adding Mandarin to the language pool would enable this in her eyes. Her chosen method of teaching, memorising Chinese poems, is a standard primary school activity in China. However, to a non-native Mandarin speaker, memorising a Chinese poem without comprehension of the meaning of each character and of the sounds of the language would be particularly difficult. What might have seemed simple to Yiyi could have seemed like a huge challenge to Alonso.

Alonso acknowledges that he should learn Mandarin, and has tried to:

Alonso: I cannot, I cannot, is too difficult the tones and also to try, I mean I try and I failed, if I have just to say a simple sentence, I can try 50 times and my parents-in-law they don't understand them my wife doesn't understand, so I am almost giving up. With Chinese, is a little bit more intimidating.

Interviewer: Why?

Alonso: Because I really feel like I fail when I try to speak, that is the bigger problem. I cannot understand myself, of course, but I cannot be understood. I would like to learn it a lot to show my wife that I'm not completely stupid, but it's difficult very difficult, especially the pronunciation. My wife speaks very standard Chinese, she could be a perfect teacher, but it's almost impossible for my mouth, to get the tones, or whatever. But every time I try, my wife says, your pronunciation is not good enough nor understandable and she's right, so yeah that is very intimidating to me. I failed, epic failure. I want a bottle of water, she was trying to say that in Italian, I was failing as usual, but she told *Voglio una bottiglia d'acqua* I want a bottle of water in Italian, it was perfect, without I told her the words in practice. Well yeah. if we were, if we had to make a competition to learn our respective native languages in two months so she would beat me and I will be still at the first I don't know. Sometimes Yiyi can switch to Italian and she can be understood by me, if I switch to Chinese it's a disaster so it's usually the communication can last for two seconds.

Despite being proficient in several languages, Alonso displays Foreign Language Anxiety (FLA) when it comes to speaking Mandarin. Despite his efforts, he feels intimidated about speaking in Chinese to his wife and with his in-laws in China, as he feels that he fails to say anything comprehensible. The fact that Yiyi speaks 'perfect' Italian also seems to make him feel inadequate. Although his wife may not intend to discourage his learning of Mandarin, her comments about his pronunciation may only be aggravating his FLA. Mandarin is a notoriously hard language to learn, as it is a tonal language with no alphabet. This is especially true for those who speak a European language as their first language. The American Foreign Service Institute organised the world's languages into four classes according to how difficult they are for an English speaker to gain proficiency in. Mandarin was placed in Class IV, alongside Arabic, Cantonese, Japanese, and Korean, as the hardest languages for English speakers to learn. These 'super hard languages' are estimated to take 2200 hours to gain proficiency in (Foreign Service Institute, n.d.). Comparatively, Italian is placed in Class I, and only 600–750 hours of learning is required to gain proficiency.

Although Alonso speaks Italian as his first language, we can presume that Mandarin is similarly difficult for an Italian speaker as English and Italian are similar languages, when one considers all the language in the world. It is thus not surprising that Alonso has found it so difficult to learn Mandarin. All the languages that Alonso knows are European languages, and Mandarin is a considerably harder language to learn. His wife, who already speaks English, has had an easier time learning Italian, which is understandable. Both Yiyi and Alonso need to have more understanding of this situation. Language learning is a slow process, especially when a European language speaker learns Mandarin for the first time. If Alonso understood that learning Mandarin takes over a year of classes to gain proficiency, he might not feel that his efforts have been in vain. More support from Yiyi could also help to reduce his FLA.

Language of Texting: He Replies in English or in Romanised Korean

In the present day, it is not only necessary for couples to be able to communicate verbally, but also in online spaces. Since the turn of the century, our lives have started to migrate online, gradually at first, then more rapidly in recent years. Since the smartphone came into widespread use, we have had online communication at our fingertips. The COVID pandemic only accelerated our virtual migration as we were forced to move our lives online. Online communication is neither spoken nor written communication. It lives according to its own rules. It is multimodal in that it contains letter words and emoji words, which can be images, videos, or sounds. Using emojis is a highly cultural decision in today's digital world. Communicating online also allows for time to quickly look up a word on Google. Even if one spouse's linguistic competence is low, they can enrich their communication with multimodal resources, such as stickers and emojis. Some of our couples met online, often as language buddies. These days you can even fall in love with an avatar. Some of our couples have spent time apart, working in different countries, and have used online communication to navigate their long-distance relationship. Knowing how to communicate in online spaces is no longer a peripheral activity: it is fundamentally needed for a relationship, intercultural or not. Online communication is important in all parts of our lives, both formal and informal. Thus, this is something that our ICs have to navigate. Many of our ICs reported employing translanguaging in digital spaces:

> Interviewer: When you text your boyfriend, do you do it in English or Korean?
> Jihye: At first, I sent him English, but now I send Hangeul too, because he has studied Korean for a year now, so I think he can follow. I send him Hangeul, and he replies in English or in Romanised Korean. I send things like "thank you" in Korean.

Jihye's husband, Alejandro, has studied Korean for a year, so Jihye and her husband mix English and Korean when they speak. Her husband reads the texts that Jihye sends in Hangeul (the Korean alphabet) and sometimes responds in romanised Korean. Texting romanised words is a form of language innovation for ICs. Although one spouse might not be able to read the orthography of their partner's first language, romanisation can help to solve the issues that might arise from this. Texting is a private space with which we all engage on a daily basis. ICs have to develop strategies to accommodate the expressiveness that they can achieve when speaking in online environments. Romanising your partner's language to make an effort to communicate with them in online spaces is another act that shows you care. It builds solidarity between a couple.

We Use Pinyin

Tony and Jane also mentioned that they use romanised forms of Mandarin to communicate:

> Interviewer: What about text messages, Chinese or English?
> Tony: A combination, but mainly Chinese, but once again it's not written characters partly because I don't I don't know many of them, and partly because I'm too lazy to try and do that properly, but we use pinyin. All of it in pinyin basically yeah.

Tony notes that they use a 'combination' of English and Mandarin, but much like their spoken language, it is mostly in Mandarin. Chinese characters are infamously difficult to learn, and so Tony uses pinyin, China's official romanisation system, to send messages to his wife using the Roman alphabet. Similarly to Jihye and her husband, Tony and Jane use innovative translanguaging practices in online spaces to achieve effective and satisfying communication.

We Can Use the Short Form

Additionally, Evelyn highlighted that she mixes English and Korean when conversing with her husband, Sanghoon. They mainly speak Korean together in daily life, but they speak some English too. Evelyn demonstrates her high proficiency in Korean, and she even knows Korean texting abbreviations:

> Interviewer: Do you text messages in Korean or English?
> Evelyn: Eh. Mix, but then it depends on the situation. If I want to speak faster, then I just type them in English. But even so, I write, in Korean, simple things like, "Where are you?" because I can use short form. Yeah I sometimes will just do that because I can save time.

Evelyn's main motivation for translanguaging in online spaces is speed of communication. This is unsurprising considering that most messaging services and apps tell us when a message has been read by its recipient, and so an uneasy type of silence can arise when we know the recipient has read our message but, for whatever reason, has not responded. This is often referred to as leaving somebody 'on read' and is generally considered rude in online communication. Compared to face-to-face silences, where one can still read the other person's expressions or body language, these online silences feel impenetrable, and can be even more hurtful if sensitive or difficult topics are involved. Evelyn thus uses English for efficiency, and Korean for simple messages, such as 'Where are you?' She also alludes to using Korean short-form texting, whereby the first letter of a syllable of a word or phrase is used, a bit like *ily* for *I love you* in English. This highlights her advanced level of Korean, as neither Tony nor Alejandro was able to use Mandarin or Korean texting language. Evelyn does not romanise her Korean messages. Instead, translanguaging practices arise from her switching between Korean and English.

Summary

The key finding of this chapter is that it is important to try to learn a new language. However, it takes a lot of time and effort. Asian languages are generally harder for European language speakers to learn and vice versa. Thus, although language is an issue for all ICs, Asian-Western couples might face greater language issues than, say, European-European ICs. Problems arise when one partner feels that their spouse has not made any effort to learn their language. This is especially the case when a couple use one partner's first language as their main language of communication or when one spouse has learnt the other's language to an intermediate level and the other spouse has not. Most partners in an IC relationship understand the difficulty of learning a new language, and they do not need or expect their partner to learn to speak their language fluently. It is simply that they would like to see some effort being made. Learning your partner's first language is an act of caring. It demonstrates that you know your partner's language is important to them and that you care about things that are important to them.

Reference

Foreign Service Institute. (n.d.). *Foreign Language Training* (no date) *U.S. Department of State.* Available at: https://www.state.gov/foreign-language-training/. Accessed November 17, 2022.

CHAPTER 3

Language of Emotion

Abstract Nelson Mandela once said, 'Because when you speak a language, English, well many people understand you, including Afrikaners, but when you speak Afrikaans, you know you go straight to their hearts'. He highlighted that sharing a language is useful for not only pragmatic meanings, but also for creating solidarity. Language carries emotion. When one does not have complete fluency in a foreign language, one of the hardest things to express is emotion.

Nelson Mandela once said, 'Because when you speak a language, English, well many people understand you, including Afrikaners, but when you speak Afrikaans, you know you go straight to their hearts'. He highlighted that sharing a language is useful for not only pragmatic meanings, but also for creating solidarity. Language carries emotion. When one does not have complete fluency in a foreign language, one of the hardest things to express is emotion.

Expressing deep emotion is closely linked to words. In some cases, there will be emotional words or phrases that are simply untranslatable into another language. Anything said in another language will thus only express half of the emotion that the spouse intends. In such instances, it can be useful for a partner to know some key emotional expressions in their spouse's language, to save them from always having to translate. Arguments are not easy even for monolingual couples, but ICs face unique challenges as one or both spouses may struggle to find the words. Sometimes, this is not even due to a lack of linguistic competence, but because of the speed at which they need to respond. This can give rise to linguistic injustice. Many couples have a designated language for arguments. This language choice needs to be carefully considered so as not to prey on the linguistic vulnerabilities of the immigrant spouse.

Many Asian languages have specific grammatical structures and particles that indicate interpersonal relations in terms of intimacy and respect. Western languages generally do not have such features (Kiaer, 2021). This can cause problems, because Asian spouses feel comfortable living within vertical systems of respect and intimacy, whilst Western spouses are used to a more horizontally friendly system. This mismatch can extend to humour and jokes too. Often humorous meanings are lost in translation, which can be difficult as humour can build solidarity within a relationship too. Couples struggle when the emotional foundation is lost. This can happen easily to intercultural couples if they only take one language as the dominant language because emotional foundations can get lost in translation. Both spouses need to make an effort to build a shared vocabulary from more than just one language. In doing so, there can be clearer communication of emotional and attitudinal meanings, leading to greater understanding and closeness between spouses.

The 3 E Model

Why do couples translanguage as they do? To understand the linguistic choices made by our interviewees, let us take a look at the 3 E Model (See Fig. 3.1). The 3 E Model was proposed by Kiaer (2021) to explain the motivations behind human communication. The 3 Es stand for efficiency,

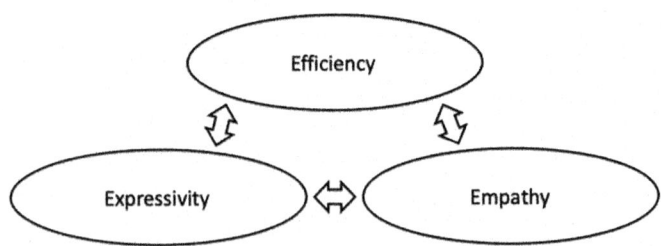

Fig. 3.1 The 3 E model

expressivity, and empathy. Our communication behaviours, such as speaking, signing, writing, and texting, are driven by the desire to make communication efficient (i.e. saving time and effort). This desire for efficiency is unconsciously encoded in our brains. We all want our intended meanings to be transmitted effectively without need for excessive explanation. As we will see later in this chapter, this often means that our couples argue in English to ensure meaning is transmitted efficiently.

Expressivity is also important in the sense that we want the underlying sentiments of our speech to be expressed clearly. Though one may be able to say something efficiently, if it does not express your sentiments of delight, anger, excitement, sadness, or whichever emotion you may be feeling, then the utterance is inherently unsatisfying. What is more, if a sentiment does not express one's emotions, then it will be inefficient by nature too. Expressivity can explain why our interviewees all mentioned needing their own languages to fully express themselves. Feelings and language are linked. We understand our feelings through language and our language through feelings. As such, many of our interviewees reported needing to swear in their own language to express frustration or anger effectively. Some feelings cannot be translated into another language, and so our interviewees translanguage for the sake of expressivity.

We also seek empathy through our language use. We use language to form and maintain bonds with others. For ICs, creating connections is closely linked to translanguaging. That is, our couples speak, write, or text using languages that are most appropriate for each situation. They consider factors such as environment, speech partners, and atmosphere, and then choose a language in order to achieve mutual understanding and empathy with the other party. The appropriate use of different languages can create a sense of emotional attachment between two speakers. It can bring a sense of belonging and empathy. In the case of our ICs, this might mean switching away from the main language that a couple uses, to their partner's or their own language. Doing this can show care for their partner and may emphasise the sincerity of what is being said.

Translanguaging Competence

As ICs spend time together on a daily basis, they hone the use of their languages with the three Es at their core. How a couple balances the three Es is their own individual choice. Sometimes it is necessary to argue one E over the others—for example, using efficient language during an argument. In this process of managing the three Es, ICs develop translanguaging competence as they build a new shared linguistic repertoire, which includes linguistic competence in both verbal and non-verbal communication. ICs manage linguistic and non-linguistic resources in a systematic yet innovative and creative manner, in order to achieve the most efficient, expressive, and empathetic mode of communication to suit the situation. That is to say, ICs not only translanguage according to linguistic competence, but also according to their environment, who is present, and the emotional atmosphere of the situation. Thus, ICs with strong translanguaging competence can mix and match language types to create the most comfortable and accommodating experience for each other, their children, wider family, and friends.

LANGUAGE OF ANGER: *COMPLETELY IN ENGLISH*

All couples encounter conflict, but having different linguistic and cultural backgrounds can provide grounds for more conflict, and more issues in resolving conflict. Thus, one of the key emotions that ICs need to navigate is anger. How to express oneself when angry and in which language is an issue unique to ICs. Conflict is, by nature, emotional, but emotions easily get lost in translation. We found that most of our ICs argue in English because it is usually the language in which both partners are most proficient:

> Interviewer: Do you argue completely in English or is some Bahasa Indonesia thrown in?
> Craig: Uh, completely in English yeah. She might occasionally throw a derogatory Indonesian word in, if she thinks I don't understand it, but yeah my Indonesian is just not good enough to understand. She's in some ways assimilated to this kind of international English environment, to the point where she said to me sometimes, if she has to read or speak like formal Indonesian she struggles, you know. She can still just switch into sort of street conversation or how she speaks with friends and family, but you know, she's not using that language and that's been the case for 11 years now.

Craig and Farah argue exclusively in English. In everyday life, they also mainly speak English, although Craig says occasionally Bahasa slips through. The ease of using English, which they are both proficient in, makes this possible. The couple make a pragmatic decision about an inherently emotional situation. It is the most logical choice. No matter which language a spouse would prefer, a couple must pick the language that they have the best mutual language proficiency in during any situation that requires negotiation.

When We Argue, of Course We Argue in English

Tony and Jane usually speak Mandarin together in their daily lives, but when they argue they also switch to English. Mandarin appeases most of Tony and Jane's communicative needs, but not their need for clear discussion during arguments:

> Jane: The funny thing is even when we argue, I mean when we argue, of course we argue in English, if I want to make sure he understands my point. But when Tony feels I am not acceding to his view, he switches back to Chinese, but uses the wrong words to explain. So I will explain again to him, you know, in this situation, you should not use that word, you should use another word and then all of a sudden, I forgot what I was arguing.

Conscious that Tony understands English better than Mandarin, Jane will switch to English when the pair is arguing. Jane feels this switch will ensure her point is being understood. Interestingly, Tony adopts the same tactic, switching to Mandarin when he feels that his point is not being accepted. Perhaps as a result of his frustration, Tony's Mandarin is not always accurate when they are arguing, and so Jane ends up correcting his Mandarin, which interrupts the flow of the argument. Though perhaps not the most effective way to resolve conflict, this dynamic change in languages demonstrates a level of care from each spouse. They try to communicate in the clearest way possible by using the language that the other is more comfortable with. Translanguaging helps convey meaning accurately and fully. As Jane said, although Chinese is the main language for their daily communication, English is the language for arguments, and from Jane's point of view, this is to make sure Tony understands her standpoint.

From Tony's point of view, speaking English helps him to feel that he can say what he really means:

> Tony: To express my sincerity, sometimes it needs English and not just because the occasion requires it, but because it's the right thing to do. There are occasions on which I use English, in order to ensure my sincerity is made clear emotionally.

Tony is in a fortunate position because Jane can speak English fluently, so he can switch to his first language to make sure that his nuance of meaning and emotion does not get lost in translation. Jane told us that she feels her first language is Korean, not Mandarin, and so she can never quite achieve the same level of emotive expression that Tony can. This once again reinforces the importance of making at least some effort to learn your partner's most comfortable language.

When He Starts Speaking in Chinese that Means He's Okay

When Tony and Jane switch back to speaking Mandarin, it signals the end of their argument:

> Jane: We want to close the chapter so we speak Chinese, like "okay what are you going to eat now?" When Tony starts speaking in Chinese that means he's okay.

During conflict, translanguaging (or the time point of language switch) serves as a discourse marker, signalling the start or the end of an argument. When one of them starts speaking English, both of them will realise that their talk has gone beyond a normal conversation and the intensity of the argument is levelled up. When either side switches back to Chinese, the other one will receive the message that it is time to move on. Through translanguaging, no one has to say sorry first to end the argument, which makes it easier to cool down an argument between the couple.

I Need Chinese to Express

Arguing in another language is not always emotionally satisfying, however. Yiyi and her husband Alonso argue in English. Their first languages are Mandarin and Italian respectively. Translation studies put a lot of emphasis on 'equivalence', that is to say, finding words of equivalent meaning and significance in another language. This is a very tricky or even an impossible feat. In crossing languages, some meaning is always lost. The lost meaning could be linguistic, cultural, or even emotional in nature. This is why arguing in another language can be so difficult and unfulfilling, as Yiyi describes below:

Interviewer: Do you argue in English completely or do you sometimes switch to Chinese?
Yiyi: I need Chinese to express.
Interviewer: But he doesn't understand though.
Yiyi: He understands I'm upset.
Interviewer: So the moment you start speaking Chinese, that's the point you're really angry.
Yiyi: Yeah yeah yeah.

Yiyi highlights that there are some things that she can only express in Mandarin. Even though her husband does not speak Mandarin, she sometimes has no choice but to speak it to release her emotions. On a verbal level, Alonso will not understand what she means. On an emotional level, however, this signals to Alonso that Yiyi is very angry. Thus, this form of translanguaging actually still allows for emotional meanings to be transmitted, even if they cannot be understood on a word level.

I Swear in Slovak

Many of our interviewees also noted that they swear in their own languages. Swearing is a very personal form of expression. It allows you to release strong emotions very quickly. As part of an IC, there will always be the language that you and your spouse are most competent in together, but having your own language is also good for your own well-being on a psychological and emotional level. There is something more satisfying about swearing in your first language, as Erika describes:

Erika: I usually swear in my head. I swear in Slovak, because it's the pronunciation. You can really emphasise it and it helps you to really express. Sometimes when I swear out loud, it's either English or Slovak depending on where I am and whether I want people to understand. But um but then sometimes when it's like when I'm caught off guard and it's like a reflex, I'm surprised so it will just be Slovak automatically.

Another of our interviewees highlighted that not being able to speak each other's languages was actually a positive in times of conflict:

Yutong: I think the good side is that because we don't speak each other's mother tongue, there's a buffer, right? You can't hurt the other person too damagingly because you know, you can't say the most vicious words in a foreign language. English is like an intermediary, so it takes the edge off.

Since Yutong doesn't speak German and her husband does not speak Mandarin; the only language they communicate in is English. Because there will always be some untranslated meaning, often emotional, an intermediary language stops any real vitriol from being transmitted from one spouse to another. Thus, there are two parts to ICs' conflicts. The first is negotiation, usually carried out in English with the pragmatic purpose of resolving an issue. The second is emotional release, which usually happens in a spouse's first language. The emotional release is often lost in translation, which can actually be useful to stop an unnecessary insult getting through to one's spouse.

Language of Resolution: *He'll Start Sending Me Texts*

Having some kind of personal space is very important for ICs. Beyond retreating into your own language, technology can also help spouses to give their partners space, as Aimee describes:

> Interviewer: If there are conflicts, how do you normally resolve them?
> Aimee: How do we normally solve problems? I think we resolve through conversation. We don't fight in an aggressive way and like he's never shouted at me. I've never shouted at him. No one's been angry. I don't think we've ever been angry and raised our voices at each other. I'm more guilty usually of giving him a silent treatment for a little while, and saying I'm processing what just happened, I'll get back to you when I'm calmer, which he doesn't like and he'll start sending me texts saying "are you okay?"

Aimee and her partner Sean speak in English together. Aimee is a native English speaker and Sean is a native Korean speaker. They do not have explosive arguments, so it seems unlikely that they explode into speaking their own languages as some of our other couples might. Nonetheless, they find their space by using technology. Sean can check in with Aimee when she is having her own space by texting her. This allows Aimee to reply in her own time, and avoid him encroaching her space. This highlights how technology can help ICs mediate conflict.

LANGUAGE OF EXPRESSION: *WE LOSE THE EXPRESSIVE CAPACITIES*

As we have seen so far, translanguaging is not purely a pragmatic choice made to improve the efficiency of communication. The use of a variety of languages can create humour, solidarity, and intimacy. It may call shared memories and experiences to mind. For example, Marcus and Erika lived in Norway before moving to Singapore, so they sometimes text using Norwegian. Their main shared language is English, so it would likely be more efficient to text using English, but it would not create the same emotional nuance. The couple also use a mix of Slovak, Malay, Mandarin, and French, though mainly just the odd phrase mixed into their English. There is no efficient reason to do this per se; it is more a matter of how the couple express themselves, as Marcus describes below:

> Interviewer: If you stopped speaking all your languages other than English as a couple, how much would English fulfil your communicative needs?
> Marcus: I think communication is not just about sharing information and getting things done. I think couples communicate because they want to grow their relationship. I think that's a very important part of the virtue and the value of communication. So if you take away all these other languages from Erika's and my relationship and it becomes strictly a monolingual one, I think the first thing I will say is we lose the expressive capacities. We will lose uniqueness, as well the uniqueness of the bond, and the fact that we can use different languages outside and chances are most people won't understand what we are saying so we get more secrecy. So we lose that part of the relationship as well, and it will just boil down to ordering things you know, like if you want to order lunch or order dinner, and then you just use English so that's quite it's quite quotidian. I think you probably end up with like 50%, of what it is now right? Because it's so rich and so diverse, yeah.

Marcus believes that only 50% of their communicative needs are met by English. From his response, it seems that the pragmatic necessities of life are discussed in English. This highlights how ICs do always have to pick one language that is useful and efficient to help them move through everyday life. Having other languages, however, adds the 'seasoning' to what would otherwise be a very bland dish. Using a few words or phrases from your partner's language can show them that you care. Using snippets of languages from other countries that you have lived in together can bring back memories of old times. Using another language in public that most people will not understand, that is, your 'secret language', can help to create solidarity between a couple. In this way, translanguaging is an expressive endeavour. It unlocks emotional nuances that might not be available in just the main language that the couple speak together.

Language of (In)Expression

Having only one language in which to communicate can thus have a limiting effect on a couple's ability to express themselves. When we asked our couples what percentage of their emotions they felt they could express in their shared language, the majority of participants said less than 100%. Most of our couples, who use English, say that it does not allow them to express their emotions, as one of our interviewees explains below:

> Interviewer: Do you think speaking English to him allows you to express all your emotions satisfyingly?
> Tallulah: I would say 90%. I'm able to express what I want to express in English, including feelings and all that, but there are just some small part that is quite difficult to yeah to express maybe 10% of the thing that I really, really want him to know is difficult to put in English for him to 100% understand it.
> Interviewer: Would you share some of the examples?
> Tallulah: Yeah mostly frustration. If I'm 100% frustrated, the way I express it, maybe he'll only feel 80% of the frustration.
> Interviewer: So when you have an argument with Manshik right, does Chinese come out accidentally sometimes?
> Tallulah: For me, no. For him, yeah, sometimes he speaks Korean.
> Interviewer: But you don't understand what he says?
> Tallulah: Yeah.

Tallulah and Manshik use English to communicate. Tallulah grew up in Malaysia, and her first languages are English and Mandarin. Manshik grew up in Korea and his first language is Korean. Tallulah's response is interesting because even though she feels that English is her first language, she still needs both English and Mandarin to express herself fully. Manshik's first language is Korean, and so sometimes when they argue, he switches to Korean to express himself, much like Yiyi. This is to be expected. The fact that Tallulah's first language is the main language used by the couple and she still feels that she is not able to express herself 100% tells us something important about being a multilingual speaker. Multilingual people learn to convey different emotional nuances in different languages, and sometimes they find that certain forms of anger, frustration, or even humour can only be expressed properly in one language. This highlights just how tricky being part of an IC can be. Though not always possible, the most expressive communication can only be achieved if both spouses know at least a bit of all the languages that their partner speaks. Marcus and Erika are a great example of this, because they both speak a little bit of lots of their languages, while English remains their main language. It is not a huge problem for Tallulah that she can only express 90% of her emotions using English; what is most important to ICs is being able to navigate the couple's pool of languages. This is something that members of an IC should make an effort to do as much as possible.

Language of Affection: *If I Want to Be Sweet, I Would Say Some Words in Italian*

Aside from anger and frustration, language is also important for expressing affection. Whether using your own language or your spouse's language, you can convey a special nuance by using either the language that is most poignant to you or the one that is most poignant to your spouse. Different languages have different uses, as Alonso describes below:

> Alonso: I use English with her if I want to make a joke. If I want to be sweet, then I would say some words in Italian to her.

Alonso's response illustrates how he uses translanguaging to evoke different feelings between himself and Yiyi. He uses English, their main shared language, to joke with Yiyi, highlighting that he sees English as their language of humour. Alonso does not speak much Mandarin, so he cannot communicate affection to Yiyi using her language. Instead, he uses his first language, Italian, to show love and care. Using your own language is a means of demonstrating sincerity and the feelings of the heart. Yiyi speaks some Italian, so the sincerity of Alonso's words likely lands well with her.

Here, we are gradually seeing how ICs have a strong awareness of their languages. This awareness of different languages and their significance within their relationships turns them into amateur linguists. Some see one language as being logical, one as more emotive, one as funnier, one as more affectionate. Each IC has a tool box from which to choose for different purposes. Monolingual couples do not have access to this form of translanguaging. ICs have strong linguistic viewpoints. It does not matter what the true linguistic reasoning is behind their views; these viewpoints simply allow them to make translanguaging work in their own unique situations.

Speaking in Korean when Trying to Wake Him up Makes it Feel a Bit Softer

As established in the previous chapter, knowing at least some of your spouse's first language is an important tool to show care. Translanguaging by mixing both spouses' first languages can unite a couple. Below, Evelyn talks about how she uses her husband's first language to show affection to him. This is a different strategy to Alonso, who uses his own first language to show affection to Yiyi.

> Interviewer: If you speak English to your husband what percentage of your communicative needs would that fulfil? And what about Korean?
> Evelyn: If I were to use English solely to communicate, I feel that I can achieve 100% of what I really want to. If I were to speak in Korean, maybe I would achieve 70%.
> Interviewer: So why do you use Korean with him then?
> Evelyn: It's like 60/40 English 40 Korean. I feel that speaking in Korea when trying to wake him up makes it feel a bit softer.
> Interviewer: So Korean is a language of emotion for you?
> Evelyn: Okay, positive wise, I will use more Korean, but when it's negative, like angry and upset, I use more English.

Evelyn's comments demonstrate how the couple balance pragmatic and emotional needs. English is a pragmatic language for Evelyn. She can communicate her meanings fully using English, which explains why she uses English when she is angry or upset. In a conflict situation, negotiation is required, and negotiation requires clear communication. To communicate with her partner affectionately, however, she chooses to use his language. When waking him up, Korean feels softer to her. Switching to Korean in these situations is a way for Evelyn to consider her and her partner's emotional needs. She can show care and consideration for her partner by using Korean at these moments. As such, Evelyn uses translanguaging for emotional purposes. She fluidly switches between languages to create different attitudinal meanings.

Language of Jokes: *Only to Be Cheeky*

Language used can also be effective to create humour. In the process of going between and beyond languages, ICs find gaps and make mistakes. They find their own ways of using each spouse's languages. In doing so, humorous use of language might arise. ICs often do not operate on 100% understanding of each other. In a sea of untranslatable and lost meanings, they make do. Often, this leads to impromptu humour. Notably, this humour might not arise from the standard humour of one culture. I have lived in the UK for over 20 years and I still do not understand British humour. Nonetheless, my husband and I still find things to laugh about. Sometimes, our humour extends from translanguaging practices, be they mistakes or creative uses of language. One of our interviewees, Craig, spoke about how he would mix Bahasa Indonesia into his English to talk to his wife playfully:

> Interviewer: Do you have a couple language? Such as mixed up languages?
> Craig: Yes. I would sometimes call her mum or mummy you know, just that kind of habit of using words that the kids use.
> Interviewer: You don't address her in any Bahasa endearment terms or anything?
> Craig: Ah, only to be cheeky.

Craig and Farah tend to talk entirely in English with each other. Farah speaks some Bahasa Indonesia with their children. From this, Craig has picked up some phrases of Bahasa Indonesia that he uses from time to time. To create humour, he sometimes uses Bahasa Indonesia terms of endearment with Farah, but this is 'only to be cheeky'. Thus, it is important to remember that translanguaging practice between IC partners can create humour, which ultimately helps unite the couple.

Language of Home: *The Language of Cuddles and Putting Them to Sleep*

Languages do not only acquire emotional meanings between two spouses in an IC; children influence the spouses' perceptions of languages, too. The times when a parent chooses to speak to a child in the couple's main language versus the times when they choose to speak in their first language can tell us a lot about the significance of each language in their lives. For example, when I speak to my children in Korean, I feel that I have more authority. When my husband and daughters speak in English, it is easy for them to dominate the conversation. When we speak Korean, it is easier for me to take my turns in the conversation. I can also use the casual Korean speech style (반말 *banmal*) with them, which helps me to feel closer to them. English lacks such developed formal and informal speech registers, so sometimes I feel that speaking English with my daughters puts more distance between us than when we speak in Korean (Kiaer, 2023). My daughter also feels that there is a noticeable difference between Korean and English. She describes English as an 'oomphy' language and Korean as a 'comfy' language, that is to say, English is a more vigorous language and Korean a softer language in her experience. English is the language that my daughter speaks at school, so she likely relates it to discipline and structure. On the other hand, Korean is a language used in home and family situations, which may explain why it feels 'comfy'. One of our interviewees also mentioned that Mandarin was a comforting language for his children and step-children:

> Nate: When Thea and the girls speak Chinese, it's the language of home. My sons spoke much more Chinese as babies, because they were with their grandma. Somehow I think it's literally the language of cuddles and putting them to sleep. They don't get many cuddles going to sleep now, but when they do or when they need it, maybe there's a bit of Chinese there. This will be true of Thea also, when they're describing things that happened in Chinese, the conversation will be in Chinese so you know they're close to their maternal grandmother. So when it's, "Oh, did you call grandma today and how is she?", they will often lapse into Chinese because they're just literally telling you what grandma said, rather than needlessly translating it.

In Nate and Thea's family, English is the main everyday language, used pragmatically to efficiently navigate the events of each day. Mandarin, however, is a language that they mostly use in the privacy of their home. It is also the language that their children use to speak with their grandmother. Therefore, English and Mandarin have taken on a different emotional significance. Nate and Thea's children have thus learnt to associate Mandarin with tender family moments. In Nate's own words, it is the 'language of cuddles and putting them to sleep'. Mandarin does have a pragmatic efficient use at times, however. Thea's daughters tend to repeat their grandmother's words in Mandarin because it is quicker and more efficient. Thus, even though one language might seem to be used for pragmatic matters more than the other, each language is flexible and can be employed dynamically. In accordance with the sentiments and emotions associated with each language, children choose when they speak in each language. In doing so, they shape their interpersonal relationships through the medium of language. As such, knowing the different emotions connected with each language is an integral part of translanguaging.

Culture and Emotion

Emotion and culture go hand in hand as much as emotion and language do. What might seem harsh in one language could seem much more respectful in another. Differences in cultures can lead to emotional misunderstandings, because each spouse is perceiving what has been said from a completely different set of cultural foundations, as Lucia describes below:

> Lucia: Sometimes the problem is not so much the language as the culture because that is the way he receives what I say. Emotional language words may be perceived differently from how I perceive them. It's the same language, so I think it's cultural.
> Interviewer: I see, so like how the word "love" is perceived?
> Lucia: Love, yes, or sadness, and exactly how we perceive it. So it's not just the language. The language is just the surface. It's the bit underneath. The way we give or the perception of the emotion.

Even though Spanish and English are comparatively closely related languages—much more closely related than, say, English and Mandarin—Lucia still perceives differences in the two languages and how she and her partner emote in those languages. Lucia's comments on this highlight the true aim of communication between ICs. It is not about perfectly combining your languages or integrating one spouse into the other's language. It is about constantly innovating to overcome the couple's differences in language, emotion, and culture. It is not a *one plus one equals two* sum, but a combining of two varied cultural linguistic backgrounds to become something totally new. Each partner enlarges their linguistic and cultural repertoire in the lifelong endeavour of understanding each other better. They create a new shared language and culture that suits their needs and those of their family. It is not about a perfect linguistic understanding, but rather a united understanding of language, culture, and emotion. Balancing these needs is one of the biggest tasks for ICs.

Summary

Language is much more than communicating information; it is also about communicating feelings. ICs may never be able to 100% understand each other's language and culture, but they still need to be able to find the optimal combination of languages to communicate their attitudinal meanings. Finding the optimal translanguaging practice is a lifelong journey. It will differ depending on location, context, speech partners, and language proficiency. Thus, although ICs might seem to be at a disadvantage by having so many languages in their repertoire, it can actually be beneficial to enrich their communication. When one language is used for one emotion and another language for a different emotion, emotional meanings can be made in a different, but not lesser, manner from monolingual couples. Being able to create emotional meanings translingually is something that ICs have to learn over time. Once they are competent in doing so, however, translanguaging can be an advantageous tool with which to communicate attitudinal meanings.

References

Kiaer, J. (2021). *Pragmatic particles: Findings from Asian languages.* Bloomsbury. (Bloomsbury studies in theoretical linguistics).

Kiaer, J. (2023). *Multimodal communication in young multilingual children: Learning beyond words.* Multilingual Matters.

CHAPTER 4

Language with the Wider Family

Abstract The linguistic and cultural differences between an IC do not just affect the two people in the couple: the couple's children, respective families, and friends are all affected too. At home, couples have to negotiate which language to speak with their children. Some couples choose to speak the language of the country that they are living in with their children, some choose to speak their L1s with their children, and some sacrifice their L1s so that the family can all communicate together. In the Kiaer family, my children spoke Korean almost exclusively until they were around four years old, meaning that my English-speaking husband was not able to communicate with them very well. This was a choice we made so that they would be able to speak both English and Korean. I know of other families, however, that chose to speak to their children in English so that both parents could communicate with their children, but this means that the children do not speak one of the parents' languages very well. Language practice at home is something that all ICs have to negotiate to suit their own unique situation.

The linguistic and cultural differences between an IC do not just affect the two people in the couple: the couple's children, respective families, and friends are all affected too. At home, couples have to negotiate which language to speak with their children. Some couples choose to speak the language of the country that they are living in with their children, some

© The Author(s), under exclusive license to Springer Nature
Switzerland AG 2023
J. Kiaer, H. Ahn, *Lessons from a Translingual Romance*,
https://doi.org/10.1007/978-3-031-32921-0_4

choose to speak their L1s with their children, and some sacrifice their L1s so that the family can all communicate together. In the Kiaer family, my children spoke Korean almost exclusively until they were around four years old, meaning that my English-speaking husband was not able to communicate with them very well. This was a choice we made so that they would be able to speak both English and Korean. I know of other families, however, that chose to speak to their children in English so that both parents could communicate with their children, but this means that the children do not speak one of the parents' languages very well. Language practice at home is something that all ICs have to negotiate to suit their own unique situation.

One of the lesser studied issues for Asian-Western couples is the in-law factor. When an intercultural couple gets together, there are not just two of them in the relationship, but all of the Asian family too. This includes not only one's parents-in-law, but also one's brother- and sister-in-law too. In-law relationships in Asia can be very challenging. On the Korean peninsula during the Joseon dynasty (1392–1897), a husband could divorce his wife on the ground that she had not been serving her in-laws properly. Incorrect treatment was known at that time as one of the 'Seven Sins' that a wife could commit. Thus, the importance of in-law relations often has its roots in custom and tradition in Asia.

There are often cultural clashes between Asian in-laws and Western spouses, as the two parties cannot always communicate particularly well. One issue that arises is how to address one's in-laws. It is not common to refer to one's in-laws by their given name in Asia. For example, in Singapore, it is typical to refer to your parents-in-law as 'daddy' and 'mummy'. Were a spouse and their in-laws to clash on this topic, however, they might find that the language barrier actually relieves the tension, as there is no way to communicate one's frustration fully. As technology improves in capability, spouses can communicate with their in-laws via texting, using Google Translate (or equivalent programmes) to help them. Although spouses and their in-laws may not be able to call each other, they can still message each other to retain some level of closeness. The in-law issue for intercultural couples highlights that IC relationships are much more complicated than one might first imagine. They involve two families and two societies, as well. This is a challenge that Asian-Western ICs face in particular.

Friends are very important for ICs too. Having groups of friends with whom they can speak their most comfortable language is a crucial way for each spouse in an IC to feel supported. Though ICs must build a good relationship between themselves and their families, it is important that each spouse has their own group of friends that they can be totally comfortable with, both culturally and linguistically. In the Kiaer family, I have found that taking my children to a Korean Saturday school every week has provided the opportunity for Korean parents to become friends and talk together. The Korean Saturday school that we went to each week was one of the largest in the UK, and so families even travelled from outside of London to go there. The school day lasted from 9 AM to 3 PM, during which time the parents would have a coffee together and chat. Usually, Korean parents are the linguistic minority in their daily lives, but at the Korean Saturday school, they became the linguistic majority. This provided the Korean parents with the opportunity to talk in their most comfortable language on a regular basis. These interactions thus became an important support network for us. Everyone has a language that they feel most comfortable speaking in, and friendship groups allow you to utilise your comfortable language. Spouses should encourage each other to make friends with people who share the same language and culture, as it enriches their everyday experience of life.

Asia, It's All about the Family

When you marry, you not only consolidate a bond between you and your partner, but also with your partner's family. Generally speaking, in-laws are relatively distant entities in Western cultures. They allow the couple to get on as they wish, even in scenarios where the in-laws may not be approving. In Asia, it is different. Families are very tight-knit, and a couple's affairs are automatically the affairs of their in-laws too. Our German participant, Stefan, described his experience with Asian in-laws as follows:

> Stefan: The family thing you know I know in in Asia family is everything, and you know back home in Germany, we are more individuals okay, but, but here in Asia, it's all about the family, in the end and it's all about how you would say respect, the honour of the family, you know. I mean it's about not losing your face and stuff like that, and in Germany, it's probably because we are too technical. We used to go every year back to her family, because my company was actually sponsoring what we call a "home trip" so it's not about the money, and you know, a flight back to Shenzhen, it's not that expensive, it's more you know, I hate to waste time on an aeroplane and

stuff. I like to stay at home, and you know go swimming. There's a pool here on the NTU campus and just to have more time for me and myself, my family instead of you know, wasting time to go somewhere where you have to wait and you know, then all these complications.

Stefan sees differences in the way family is viewed between the two cultures. He believes his wife, Yutong, focuses more on family and her parents, while he values independence. He believes that Yutong wanting to go back to China every Lunar New Year takes too much time and effort. He would rather spend time being by himself or with his immediate family, meaning himself, his wife, and his daughter.

Meeting the In-Laws

Meeting one's in-laws is a daunting occasion for anyone, but for ICs, simply telling them about your partner can be worrying. Once you reach the age of 25, Asian parents and older relatives begin to ask you when you are getting married. Many Asian parents prefer that their child marry someone of the same ethnic minority. They also prefer, if you are female, that you marry someone older than you. This is related to power dynamics both within the family and society. It is often seen that being with someone older is more beneficial for your position in society. It is also seen as the norm, as the husband tends to have more authority in the household, so an older age matches this idea. Below, Jane recounts telling her parents that she was in a relationship with an English man:

> Jane: My parents, especially my dad, were really, really strict to my sisters. My dad didn't approve of Han Chinese partners. He told my sister that you can only marry Korean, so they all married Koreans, and they all got divorced. They were not happy, so I guess my dad already gave up. When I was studying UK, they also told me do not date British guys or foreigners at all, so actually before I met my husband Tony, I never had any boyfriend because there was no chance for me to meet anyone because I know that my parents anyway, they will disapprove, so I didn't even try it. When I met Tony in China in the office, I was almost 27, 28 years old. At the time, my parents started asking me, "do you have a boyfriend?", "when are you going to get married?" So when I met Tony, I didn't tell my parents, because I didn't know how they were going to react. So yeah because, but I was actually quite pressured by them. One day, and after I hung out with Tony for three months or two months, I forgot, I told them. I called my Dad. I was

so nervous. I told my dad, "I have a boyfriend now" and then I said, "he is my colleague, he is British". Although he's actually almost four years younger than me I couldn't tell him, so I said that we are the same age. My dad was really quiet on the other end, and I was so nervous, I was in Beijing. And then he said, "Okay, as long as you're happy". Oh my God, I was so surprised, then I realised that because of all my sisters, all those marriage horrors, yeah made my parents feel like they should not intervene.

Jane has conservative parents who care greatly about the ethnicity and age of her partner. This is a big issue in diaspora families. Parents from ethnic minority groups often want their children to marry those of the same ethnicity to keep their ethnic identity. This is particularly important to the Korean diaspora, who consider Koreans to be a homogenous race of people. However, Asian parents tend to be more agreeable to intercultural marriage when a partner is Western. Marrying an Asian person of a different Asian race is especially alarming to Asian parents, due to prejudicial beliefs. In the West, marriage is an individual decision with which parents tend not to interfere. In Asian societies, however, one's mother, father, and even siblings are all entitled to an opinion. One's marriage must be agreeable to many members of the family in Asia. If even one person is unhappy, it can break the family relationships. As such, intercultural couples do not enter into marriages as individuals; family and society are involved too. Even if the couple themselves are not having any individual issues, there might be familial or societal issues affecting their relationship.

Notably, our interviews found that most Western parents were very accepting of their child's spouse. Lucia's mother, who is Spanish, was very welcoming of Manny from the moment that they met:

Manny: When I met Lucia's mom for the first time, it was funny because we had to fly to Spain at different times. I had to go first and she had to come one day after. Can you imagine meeting your future mother-in-law without your then-girlfriend and now-wife? I was alone, but open arms, she accepted me with open arms, with no problem.

In his interview, Manny described worrying about what his parents would think of Lucia because his family is strongly religious. He mentioned that his father was also a little dubious, like Jane's, but he soon came around. In comparison, Lucia's mother, who is Spanish, had no qualms about Manny. She accepted him with 'open arms'. As we will see throughout this chapter and the next, Western parents strongly believe in giving their children freedom to choose and respecting their decision. Who you marry is a personal decision in the West, while it can be seen as more of a family decision in Asia. It is, however, great to see that both Jane's and Manny's parents accepted their spouses despite their different ethnicities. It is important to remember that Asian families can be flexible too.

Addressing the In-Laws: He Uses 'Eomma', 'Appa', but I Never Called His Parents 'Mom 'Dad'

In most Asian languages and cultures, it is rare to ever call your parents-in-law by their names. Calling someone by their name is seen as something done by equals. Parents are always above their children in Asian hierarchies, and so it is unheard of for sons- or daughters-in-law to call their parents-in-law by their names. Many of our interviewees spoke about this:

> Interviewer: How does he address your parents?
> Jane: That's the funny thing. In the beginning he was asking me what's your dad's name, what's your mom's name? I told them can I call them ma'am misses, no. I said okay call them "eomma, appa". So when he calls my parents, he calls "eomma, appa", but I never called his parents mom dad.

In Korean culture, it is of the utmost importance to show respect to your parents-in-law. Korean has a phrase, *dongbang yeui ji gook*, which literally translates to *the respectful land to the east*, referring to Korea. Despite no longer claiming to be a Confucian country, Korea still takes the concept of filial piety very seriously, alongside many other Neo-Confucian norms that were widespread in Korea from the sixteenth to nineteenth century. Jane's parents are ethnically Korean, although they live in China. In Korea, it is common to refer to your mother-in-law as *eommeonim* (mother + honorific particle *nim*) and your father-in-law as *abeonim* (father + honorific particle *nim*). Thus, when addressing Jane's parents, Tony does not use English or Chinese—the two languages he speaks on a daily basis – but adopts the Korean terms. He follows Asian norms to call them mom and dad, although he omits the conventional -*nim* suffix, which is added to show greater respect. Nonetheless, his willingness to adopt a third language to refer to them is positive and shows Jane's parents that he is making an effort. Interestingly, Jane didn't force herself to change her cultural habits and address Tony's parents with their names, as this sounds impolite from her own cultural lens. She also did not force herself to call them mom and dad, as most Asian people do, because she was not comfortable with it. She finally compromised by not addressing them directly. This means that there is great freedom in terms of language choice in this family and there are no stringent rules in language use, which, again, reflects the spirit of translanguaging.

I Don't Call Them Anything

Another of our participants, Nate, also mentioned avoiding calling his parents-in-law anything:

> Nate: So, I mean the interesting thing is, I think I've only met them two or three times because we never lived in Taiwan, and this is a four or five, six-year relationship, not a 20 year one. I don't know why, I call them Grandpa sort of Chinese words or Taiwanese words for Grandma and Grandpa because everyone else is calling them. Because usually if I'm seeing them or it's on a video call, the girls are talking to them and Thea's talking to them with the girls there and it's kind of a group conversation, and so, when Thea is talking to them with the girls, she'll call them Grandma and Grandpa. When the girls are talking to them, they'll call them Grandma and Grandpa, I just use that term. Individually if it's just Thea and I with them, I actually don't call them anything, deliberately. Traditionally, I guess, this would have been the case previously. The expectation is that you will call them Mom and Dad, which I just find that I would do when required.
> Interviewer: Mom and dad grandma grandpa in Chinese Taiwan Chinese.
> Nate: Yes.
> Interviewer: I see and then, when it becomes you two, you avoid.
> Nate: I avoid, yeah. I tap on the shoulder or just start talking. Quite common across you know, sons-in-law we usually use the term and I have no, I have no objection to doing it, but it just feels so…
> Interviewer: You don't call them by their name.
> Nate: No, definitely wouldn't, don't even know the dad's name.

Nate has only met Thea's parents two or three times because they have only been together five or six years as a couple and they have never lived in Taiwan together. Nate addresses them with the Chinese terms for grandmother and grandfather, mostly because that is what everyone else calls them. When they are on video calls with the in-laws, he calls them grandma and grandpa, but when it's just himself and Thea with her parents, he avoids addressing them directly. He says normally he would be expected to call them mum and dad but he finds that a bit strange so he just avoids the issue. Nate says that if he did have to address them as mum and dad he would do so. He does not use their given names as it would be rude and he doesn't even know what they are.

I Call Her Mummy

All Asian countries have some form of polite address term by which one refers to their in-laws. There are microvariations between the countries. In Singapore, it is common to refer to your boyfriend's or girlfriend's parents as *aunty* and *uncle* before marriage. Once you are married, it is common to refer to your spouse's parents as *mummy* and *daddy*. This does not match exactly with other customs of address in other Asian languages and cultures. Below, Bob, a Korean man, describes the clash he felt between Korean and Singaporean address terms:

> Interviewer: How do you address your girlfriend's parents?
> Bob: I just call her "mummy". Usually, you would call them *aunty* and *uncle*, but that seems like calling them *ajeossi* and *ajumma*, which doesn't seem okay to me. So, I call her *mummy*.
> Interviewer: What about her dad?
> Bob: I don't talk with her father as much.

In Korean society, it is important to show respect to your significant other's parents. This is achieved through a range of verbal and non-verbal strategies (Kiaer, 2023). The need to show this respect extends from the Confucian concept of filial piety, which gained great traction in Joseon Korea, and has lingered in the society ever since. Using an appropriate address term is thus very important to Korean people. As aforementioned, it is most common to refer to your in-laws as *eommeonim* (mother + honorific particle *nim*) and your father-in-law as *abeonim* (father + honorific particle *nim*) in Korea, no matter whether you are married or not. To Bob, *mummy* and *daddy* are the Singaporean equivalents of *eommeonim* and *abeonim*. *Aunty* and *uncle*, however, are the equivalents of *ajeossi* and *ajumma*. *Ajeossi* and *ajumma* are two terms that could be likened to *Mr* and *Mrs* in English. They tend to refer to someone who is at least one generation older than you, but they do not contain any strong sentiment of respect. They can be neutral or derogatory terms depending on the context, and they are often used to refer to strangers. In Singapore, *aunty* and *uncle* are similar terms in that they can be used to refer to those older than you, but that is really where the likeness ends. Bob, however, equates *aunty* and *uncle* with *ajeossi* and *ajumma*, which are not respectful terms. Therefore, he feels it would be strange to call his girlfriend's parents *aunty* and *uncle*, as it would not be respectful enough.

Communicating with the In-Laws: *He Makes a Lot of Effort to Speak in Slovak*

When it comes to verbal encounters in intercultural settings, words do not matter as much as one's intentions. Erika describes how her Singaporean husband makes an effort to speak to his in-laws in Slovak, even though he is not fluent:

> Interviewer: When Marcus speaks to your family members, what's the language?
> Erika: So he'll try to make a lot of effort and speak in Slovak, especially to my grandparents because they don't understand English. But if it's becoming more complex, then he'll call me and he'll say, can you translate? And then I'll translate.

Making this effort is a very good first step in establishing a positive relationship with your in-laws. Even if he cannot say everything, Marcus demonstrates a willingness to connect with his wife's family, which is almost more important than being able to have fluent discussions with them. His openness to a new language highlights his desire to participate in, and learn about, Erika's language and culture. Thus, Marcus making an effort to speak Slovak is important not only to his in-laws, but also to his wife. Making an effort to get along with in-laws can bring a couple closer together.

They Can't Drop the Subtle Hints

In Asia, it is expected that you accept your in-laws as your family. This is not necessarily as ubiquitously true in Western couples. The Asian tendency can create a lot of tension because it can seem burdensome. Asian families get involved in lots of decisions that would be individual to the couple in the West. This can be annoying and upsetting to those of Western heritage. If your spouse cannot speak the same language as your parents, however, communication will be limited. In our sample, there are hardly any couples where both spouses can communicate properly with their in-laws. That said, the communication gap can be considered a blessing at times. Lack of linguistic skill gives each party some space, resulting in less conflict. If my husband could speak good Korean or my mother English, then they would likely get into arguments easily. Thus, I am grateful that they don't speak each other's languages efficiently. This does, however, put stress on the mediator/translator. They constantly need to negotiate and mediate to try to make the situation work for all parties. In the Kiaer family, my father does not speak much English and my husband does not speak much Korean. When they wish to converse, I translate for them. Ultimately, I end up making up some bits of what they say to avoid any conflict from their cultural differences. I would say my translations are 20% and 80% my own additions. I meditate not only linguistically but also emotionally. In fact, I feel that the emotional mediation might even be more important than the linguistic mediation, Below are two comments from our participants who do not speak the language of their parents-in-law:

> Nate: One helpful aspect is you know, conversations about when are you guys getting married or this kind of thing, is great because of the language limitation. They don't have those conversations with me and they can't drop the subtle hints because I well, I would rather not get the subtle hints or I could easily pretend not to get the subtle hints. And no one would ever ask directly, so that's a helpful aspect.
>
> Stefan: You know I always make some point, you know actually I'm a very happy husband, because I don't speak the same language, like my parents in law, you know, then you know, for example, whenever you know my mother-in-law is angry, you know she will not be able to communicate that.

Both Nate and Stefan are relieved that they cannot communicate fully with their parents-in-law. Although they might be able to speak some pleasantries in their language, the communication does not go beyond this, and so they cannot have discussions on more serious topics. Language barriers are typically considered negative, but in these cases, the language barrier between spouse and in-laws creates space and helps to stop conflict arising.

There Are Times when Colin Is Rude to Them

Colin and Aliyah were one of the few couples that we interviewed who a) could both communicate with their in-laws well in English and b) have lived in the same country as their in-laws. Colin and Aliyah first met in Melbourne, Australia, when Aliyah was studying there. At the time, Aliyah's parents were also living and working in Melbourne for part of the year. Unlike some of our other couples, this meant that Colin had spent a lot of time around his in-laws, leading to conflict between them, as Aliyah describes:

> Aliyah: When my parents come here to Melbourne, I mean Colin is very respectful of them on so many levels, but there are times when Colin is rude to them, like, I would not do that to Colin's parents. I wouldn't do that because I've been raised to respect elders in a particular way. Because of my Asian upbringing, I think. Colin gets annoyed with his parents and he treats his parents like that, too. At times, when they come to his house, he's rude to them as well. And I had, that upsets me because like, dude they drove all the way from Adelaide, you get upset over one little thing, and you just slam a door and walk out. And now we see these things in Rose. Rose slams the door and when Colin gets upset, I asked him, "how can you get upset?" These are learned behaviours, she has seen you slam a door and walk out on your parents, and you're getting upset by a seven-year-old or eight-year-old slamming it on you.

Here, Aliyah's Sri Lankan upbringing, which emphasises respect towards elders, clashes with Colin's behaviour. Likely, Colin's behaviour would be considered rude both from an Asian and Western point of view, but Aliyah feels Colin's behaviour would be completely unacceptable in Sri Lankan culture. Aliyah finds this even more worrying as their daughter has started to act in a similar way. This means that her Sri Lankan culture is not being passed on to her daughter, which is worrying for her.

LIVING WITH IN-LAWS

The tight-knit nature of Asian families means that it is common for couples to live with their parents-in-law, especially at the start of their relationship. In comparison, couples would rarely ever live with their Western in-laws. Western parents often want their children to go out and start their own lives. They put a lot of value on independence, as Stefan describes below:

Stefan: But see you know in Germany it's different because you want to be independent, you know actually your parents want to see you step away, you leave the house and can build up your own family and be on your own know, and I think this is, this is one of the typical differences between Asians and Westerners. For me it's always important to be independent and, of course, my parents don't want me to help them all the time, because they want to prove themselves that they can do it on their own, and they don't need the help. That's a big difference because Yutong was, for example, in contact with her parents every day, you know, calling and stuff like that so. And, and our culture is different in Germany.

Living with one partner's parents can, however, have great economic benefits. Asian parents seldom ask their children to pay rent to live with them, so couples are able to save up money to buy their own place. However, when ICs live with their in-laws, clashes can arise, as Aliyah describes below:

Interviewer: Did Colin have an issue with your parents at the beginning, you know, because of different expectations as a parent-in-law or son-in-law or anything like that?
Aliyah: He came to live with us for 1 year, so we could collect money to buy our house, it was a very hard period. It was very, very hard for him, but I think it was very hard for my parents as well. Colin and my mom are not easy people to live with.
[…]
Aliyah: In subcontinental cultures [in Asia], there are no boundaries. Anyone can walk anywhere into any space, because there are no boundaries. When Colin moved in, I gave him my study. My mom and dad and I secretly used to joke that with Colin, it's like the three of us were living in his house. We felt very worried that we would upset him, we would get in his space because initially, for the first few months that he was there, my mom used to suddenly walk into the study and he used to get upset. And that's why they decided to go back to Sri Lanka for a few extra months. He would be in his study working and my mom would come and open the door and say, "come for lunch". If you live in the same house there's no knocking on the door, "may I please", none of that. That's formal so it's a sign of distance.

Aliyah highlights that Colin's relationship with her parents was very rocky at the start. They stayed with them during the first year of their marriage to save money for their own house. However, Colin could not acclimatise to the lack of boundaries and personal space which apply in

Sinhalese culture. Colin is very reclusive and wants his privacy. He argued with her mother and they argued amongst themselves while living in her parents' house, to such an extent that Aliyah's parents left their house in Melbourne and went to Sri Lanka earlier than usual (they spend time in Sri Lanka every year to get away from the Melbourne winter). Aliyah can see that it was very big-hearted of her parents to let them keep living there, even though it was not going smoothly. This courtesy might not have been afforded to them by Western parents.

THE MIRACLE OF TECHNOLOGY

Anyone who had to communicate internationally before 2000, or perhaps even 2010, will remember the pain of making international calls. When I first came to the UK, I had to buy an international calling card to make phone calls to my friends and family in South Korea. These could be as expensive as £50 per card. I remember the effort that I had to make to first acquire the card, then find the right area code to make the call, then wait for the call to connect, and then deal with a crackly line and poor volume. Each call would be very lengthy to justify the effort and expense. I had no other choice though, as the only other option would have been to send a letter, which would have also been expensive and very slow.

At the time, international flights were very expensive too, especially for those making a new life in a new country. As such, moving to another country was an isolating experience, as it was so difficult to communicate with family and friends in another country. Then, Skype came along and revolutionised our communication capabilities. Skype was founded in 2003, although it may not have been widely used at the time. As computers, internet connections, and eventually smartphones became staples in our lives, we were able to instant message, voice call, and video call our relatives abroad.

The first time I made a video call, I was amazed! It allowed me to feel much more closely connected to my friends and family in Korea. Even though the physical distance was the same, I could bridge the gap virtually—something that was unimaginable to me when I first moved to the UK. This has proved invaluable for maintaining bonds between my children and their family in Korea too. My parents have witnessed my children growing up through video calls and pictures that I have sent to them via KakaoTalk (the most popular instant messaging service in South Korea). Were they born a decade or two earlier, they would have only been able to speak with their grandparents via phone from time to time. My parents would have hardly known what they looked like! Thanks to the miracle of technology, my children chat with their Korean family regularly. We even attended my cousin's wedding on Zoom during the pandemic, something that I would never have believed possible 10 or 20 years ago. Increased technological capabilities have helped to hugely ease the burden of leaving one's country. They reduce the isolation that immigrant spouses may experience.

COMMUNICATING WITH IN-LAWS: *IF I HAD A LOCAL MOTHER-IN-LAW, SHE PROBABLY WON'T BE SO EXPRESSIVE*

Advances in technology do not only mean that immigrant spouses can stay connected with their family; immigrant spouses' partners are also able to connect with their in-laws. When a spouse and their in-laws were not proficient in the same languages in, say, the 1990s, it seemed like a waste of money and effort to have them talk on the phone, beyond just saying a quick hello. Video chat functions, online translators, and multimodal messaging capabilities all help spouses and their in-laws to communicate around language barriers. This means that positive relationships with in-laws can be established across borders, as Charlie describes below:

> Interviewer: I guess his mother really likes you because you speak Korean.
> Charlie: Yes. She doesn't have any girls, only two boys, so maybe she likes. She always sends me very nice messages like we have a cuddle chatting back and then she was like send "I should be there for you there". Koreans, one thing that I find very different from Singaporeans or other countries, is like their expressions tend to be very slightly like extreme, like they describe something like sharing or something that would be like "Oh, we share like from the bottom of our heart as a community", like they tend to emphasise their expressions, that I'm not really sure how to and also sometimes like when I want to translate it into English, it feels very like it feels very like not overwhelming. Like, just a simple thank you, but in Korean, it will sound like, "thank you for saving my life", you know that kind of impact is very different.
> [..]
> Charlie: They'll always express their thankfulness and stuff, like "Oh, thank you for raising the children. It must be so tough on you" that kind of thing.
> [...]

Charlie: I feel like, if I have a local mother-in-law, she probably won't be so expressive. Maybe it is also because, like we are not there, maybe she misses them a lot also, that's why she, that's why her expression is so. That's why, whenever I read the messages, that now I'm thinking, maybe I should really go there, because they are quite old already, about 60 and 70.

Charlie has a positive relationship with her mother-in-law, with help from technology. This in turn is helped by that fact that Charlie speaks Korean well, and likely also that John's mother never had a daughter of her own. All their text messages are very loving, with many kisses and so on. Charlie thinks that her mother-in-law is more expressive because she is Korean, and she wouldn't expect a Singaporean mother-in-law to be so intense. Charlie thinks that John's mother misses her grandchildren a lot and this makes Charlie question whether she is being selfish in not agreeing to move to Korea. She says that her mother-in-law is extremely positive and encouraging in every way. John does not contact his mother or his brother very often and Charlie thinks it's because he is embarrassed that he doesn't have a job and they may nag him about this.

NAMING CHILDREN

Choosing your child's name is important for any couple. However, in Asian cultures, this can be an issue in which your parents and grandparents are involved. Naming can represent cultural value systems. In Asian families, this means valuing the wishes of your parents and grandparents, even if they go against your own ideas. In the Kiaer family, my niece's name was not decided until a whole month after she was born, as my father (her grandfather) would not approve of the name that my brother/sister had chosen for her. In Korea, family registers are typically held under the grandfather's name. This means that you need the approval of the grandfather to register a child's name. In the West, when you think about the head of a family, you often think about the parents in a nuclear family. In Korean families, however, it is the grandparents who are the head of the family. Therefore, the grandfather has a large amount of influence over his grandchildren's names. In this way, naming reveals the power structures at play in Korean society.

My Mother Gave Her the Name. I Hated that Name

In Chinese culture, naming also involves the parents. The choice of names sometimes stems from a generation poem, meaning that one character from the poem will be taken for each generation. In such instances, Chinese names are formed as follows: family name + generation name + given name. This is a traditional practice that does not happen in all families. Generally speaking, however, names are seen as very important in Chinese culture, and grandparents often want their grandchildren to have auspicious names, so they want to be involved in the naming process. Below, Yutong describes how her mother chose a Chinese name for her daughter that Yutong did not like:

> Yutong: Zhou is her middle name. It's all for legal pragmatism, because I was concerned if there's a time when I, for example, travel along with her, how do I prove I'm her mother right? And I add that as her middle name. Her Chinese name is Zhou Ziyu.
> Interviewer: Zhou Ziyu..
> Yutong: My mother gave her the name. I hated that name, but I accepted it anyway.
> Interviewer: But was Stefan okay with getting a name from your mom?
> Yutong: I think he doesn't care.
> Interviewer: And do you use her Chinese name at all?
> Yutong: Paige's Chinese name?
> Interviewer: Yeah.
> Yutong: Not really, it's on her birth certificate but I seldom call her it.
> Interviewer: But when you didn't like her name, why did you still use it then?
> Yutong: Because you haven't met my mom. She's very beautiful, she's very powerful, and she's also a professor of Economics. She's the ultimate matriarch of not just my family, but a whole clan and she's a superstar of our university, she's a very powerful woman.
> Interviewer: I see.
> Yutong: I already disappointed her with the wedding so I wouldn't dare to disagree with her about the name.

Yutong has to juggle being married to a German man whilst also being the daughter of a powerful and traditional Chinese mother. Despite the fact that she did not like the Chinese name that her mother chose for her daughter, she just accepted it as she felt she had already disappointed her mother enough by having a small wedding (more on this in Chap. 5). Yutong conceded on this point to keep her mother, who she describes as the 'ultimate matriarch', happy. This highlights how ICs have to make sacrifices and concessions. If you do not follow the Asian parents' wishes on one matter, then you will likely need to appease them by conceding to them on another occasion. Interestingly, it was not Stefan who clashed with his in-laws in this instance; rather it was Yutong who clashed with her own parents.

Sometimes My Wife Would Worry about How They Would Be Perceived Overseas

Even though it is customary for Indonesian parents to get involved in naming their grandchildren, Craig and Farah did not involve Farah's parents. This, once again, was Farah's choice:

> Craig: That's not something I really thought of, but I guess the tradition of my family has been followed so they've taken my surname, which is not one I'm particularly attached to. So you know, again it's something I look back on now and I wondered whether we needed to do that, whether we could have thought of other ways, but we gave them an English first name and Indonesian middle name and they took my family name. Because we're outside of Indonesia so again the conventions of Hong Kong and Singapore was to have a family name and a first name so it's partly my culture, but it's also part of the places we were living, you know, in the legal conventions. Sometimes my wife would worry about how they would be perceived overseas, so she might be the one that actually insisted on a Western surname, because she wants to ensure that that they can you know, grow up in, say New Zealand, and have a you know, and have an experience that's similar to what other New Zealanders have.
>
> Interviewer: Who was involved in a naming process? Just only you two or family members?
>
> Craig: Yes, yes, just us. Um, I think traditionally grandparents would have a role in Indonesian culture, but like my wife does not trust her parents.
>
> Interviewer: In terms of?
>
> Craig: She has a very specific idea, she's a modern person. I think she wouldn't have liked something. Actually, that's really interesting. I can't give you a good answer as to why she doesn't like it. It's just she wouldn't

accept what her parents had chosen for her. Um maybe that's part of her independence as a child, partly why she ended up marrying a foreigner and leaving Indonesia is that she has a strong personality.
Interviewer: Would you be okay that her parents be part of?
Craig: I think I would have been more okay.

Upon being asked about his children's names, Craig realised for the first time that they had followed a non-traditional Indonesian naming style, with the children taking his family name. Craig highlights an important point, however: that names are not just affected by parents and grandparents, but also where you reside. The couple ended up giving their children names that followed the legal naming practices of Singapore and Hong Kong. As an IC, Farah seems to be particularly aware of their family's international nature. Thus, Craig mentions that Farah wanted to give them Craig's Western surname so that they would 'fit in' in New Zealand. Craig describes Farah as being independent and not wanting to accept what her parents would have chosen for her, so she likely values being a global citizen over being an Indonesian citizen, therefore choosing to forgo Indonesian traditions. Through their naming practices, Farah is also passing down these sentiments to her children.

A Cross-Cultural Relationship Gave us a Free Pass

Another of our couples, Nate and Thea, also found that being in an IC meant that Thea's parents did not get involved in naming their grandchildren:

Interviewer: When you naming your two boys when they are born, or if you have a child between you and Thea, did you involve your family in naming the children's process or only happened between you two or?
Nate: Obviously it wasn't it wasn't the same too, but no we didn't involve family which was no problem, but was different from the norm. I would genuinely see it in both relationships, the fact that it was a cross cultural relationship gave us a free pass for a lot of things rather than, probably I presume, there are some intercultural couples who do things exactly the way that one culture would expect, but because they're an intercultural couple, they can never get it right. I would almost feel the opposite, we can never get it wrong because people give us leeway. With Andrew and Andy, there was no involvement, but it was important to both of us that the names worked in both languages. So both of their Chinese names have been, Andrew's *Andelu*, and Andy's *Andi*, easily transliterated, if that's the right

word, which means you know, their Chinese grandma calls them a very similar sounding name to my grandma, and that was that was important in the names.

ICs live between and beyond the boundaries of culture, as Nate aptly describes, saying, 'We can never get it wrong'. His in-laws are actually more understanding because he and Thea are an IC. Instead of considering what their parents would think of their grandchildren's names, Nate and Thea chose names that could be easily pronounced by both sets of grandparents. This is considerate towards Andrew and Andy too, as might help them to feel attached to both sides of their cultural identity.

Talking with Children

When we asked our interviewees about the languages that they speak at home with their children, we found that many of our participants felt their language could be burdensome for their children. Some interviewees felt that speaking too many languages with their children would confuse them. This is an attitude that we have encountered frequently throughout our work in linguistics and child multilingual language development. There is, however, no evidence that living in a multilingual setting will negatively affect a child's cognition. Foreign Language Anxiety is the only possible issue that could arise, but this only happens when children are forced into artificial immersion environments. For example, Foreign Language Anxiety is prevalent in Korean children who are sent to English classes at a young age, when they do not speak any English at home. Comparatively, Foreign Language Anxiety is unlikely to arise in multilingual households, as children feel safe and at ease around their parents. Thus, instead of reducing the number of languages spoken at home for your child's sake, it is actually better for parents to speak whichever language feels most natural to them in the moment. If a parent is able to speak comfortably, then it will help their child to feel comfortable too. Children's brains will naturally sort out the rest, so long as they are not put under any pressure. The idea that multiple languages pose a cognitive burden for children is a common myth that would be better off left in the past.

One of our interviewees, John, who has struggled with speaking English in Singapore, spoke about not wanting to speak Korean with his children so as not to make them struggle to learn two languages:

Interviewer: Why do you not speak Korean with your children?
John: I had such difficulty in learning English, and I don't want my children to suffer like me, so I speak with them in English. My wife complains to me saying, "Why don't you speak Korean to them as you are Korean!" But I want them to learn English as fast as they can, so they don't have the trouble that I have.

Although John speaks Korean to his wife, he wants his children to speak good English, so he chooses not to speak to them in Korean. As a result, his children speak little Korean. In reality, this not something that John needs to worry about, because Charlie, his wife, speaks English and his children go to school in English. Speaking Korean at home with their father would not hinder them from learning English. John does not want his children to suffer from not being able to speak English as he did. He projects his experience onto his children unnecessarily, but he does so with good intentions.

Tip box: Artificially reducing the number of languages that you speak with your children is not necessary. Simply speak whichever languages feel most natural to you in the moment, and their linguistically adept brains will work them out.

It's a Small Language, so It's Not So Important

One of our participants, Erika, speaks about her experience with raising a child in a multilingual household. She is a native Slovak speaker, but her husband speaks English, and they live in Singapore.

Interviewer: Why do you feel it's so important for him, do you think it's important for him to learn Slovak? Why?
Erika: Um. No actually. Because it's a small language so it's not so important, I mean, but I think it's important on a personal level that my son can communicate with my family, so he can connect better. I think it would be so weird if you know, if the mummy is Slovak, and he doesn't speak Slovak. And also, I think it's good just in general for the brain. Then later, it will be easier for him to pick up some languages. It's easier right, when you think of grammar and syntax and so on, it kind of shows him a different perspective.

Erika shows a very healthy attitude towards child multilingual language acquisition. She doesn't think that learning Slovak is a necessity for her child, though she can see a lot of benefits of learning it, such as better communication with her family in Slovakia, cognitive benefits of being multilingual, improving language learning strategies, and seeing things from multiple perspectives. This likely indicates that she doesn't put a lot of pressure on her son to learn Slovak perfectly, which often leads to better language acquisition (Kiaer, Morgan-Brown, Choi, 2021). It seems that Erika doesn't relate language to power and she leaves the freedom of language learning to her son. This suggests that in Erika's mind, languages are not exclusive of each other, but constitute a speaker's whole linguistic repertoire, which is in line with translanguaging theory.

It's Mostly for Them to Learn about the Culture

Another of our interviewees, Farah, speaks in Bahasa Indonesia with her children. Her motivations are more cultural than linguistic.

> Interviewer: Your children, I know you have two, but what are their languages like?
>
> Farah: So they mainly speak English, but I speak to them 50–50 in English and in Bahasa because my parents don't speak English, so I now want them to connect with their grandparents and in that level where they can understand each other, so yeah they mostly speak English at home.
>
> Interviewer: When you say 50–50, which kind of area do you speak to them in Bahasa Indonesia and what topics do you switch to English or do you have that subconsciously or is it subconscious or conscious effort?
>
> Farah: I'm when I'm telling them off or when I'm you know reprimanding them I'm using English more. But in in like a very casual way and we're when we're joking around or just messing around with each other, we use Bahasa. When we greet each other in the morning I use Bahasa and yeah if I if it's just random it's not really I can't really say like which area I would use Bahasa it's just like when I feel like doing always speaking Bahasa, then I will do that and yeah sometimes when I get upset as well, I will just like blurt out some Bahasa yeah.
>
> Interviewer: What's the role of Bahasa in your family?
>
> Farah: I think it's mostly for them to learn about the culture, to understand values so for the cultures that that we have, especially as I was brought up as a in Javanese household, mostly Javanese household, like what is rude, what is impolite and yeah I think that's quite important.

Farah's response highlights a very important feature of IC families: conflict rarely arises about linguistic competence. Verbal encounters matter, but the attitude and manners that you use matter more. These aspects of communication stem from cultural understanding, rather than linguistic competence. Speaking Indonesian with her children is a way to ensure they have an understanding of Indonesian culture, rather than the language being purely a mode of communication.

They Could Easily Lose Their Chinese Heritage

Another of our interviewees spoke about the importance of his children learning their heritage language, Mandarin, whilst they are living in Singapore and speaking mainly English:

> Interviewer: So in your family, Chinese plays a very important role, even if you speak exclusively in English you, it seems like Chinese language in your family plays quite an important role, what do you think?
> Nate: Yes, of course, it was yeah and I think that's, for you know for Thea and the girl, they arrived as a kind of ready set Taiwanese family. And they have no, they have no doubt about that. I guess five, 10, 15 years down the line, they may look at this period as being a cultural adjustment period, but they arrived as native Chinese speakers and also because they look Chinese. With the boys, I think it's a different type of importance because it's important to their cultural heritage in a way that could easily be lost. With the boys, they could easily lose their Chinese heritage. So it's more important to keep it there.
> Interviewer: So you think it's very important for them and for you to keep Chinese language, do you think?
> Nate: Yes, I think so. They study it in school so it's important for them to kind of keep that up.

Similar to Farah, Nate highlights that speaking Mandarin is important so that they do not lose their cultural heritage. He compares his sons to Thea's daughters. Thea's daughters grew up in Taiwan, so they already have a strong Taiwanese cultural identity. His boys have a Chinese mother, but they have lived in Singapore, so there is a risk of them losing their connection to their Chinese heritage. In Nate's mind, learning Mandarin can help them to maintain cultural links to China. Even though Nate is not Chinese himself, he is trying to ensure that his children remain connected to their heritage. Interestingly, he also views learning Mandarin as an academic pursuit that his children should do well in too.

> **Tip box:** There is no use in trying to make your child grow up like a child from your home country. Instead, give them the opportunity to explore both parents' languages and cultures. This will enrich their understanding and overall life experience. This will help them to develop a multicultural identity, which will stem from your family as a whole, rather than one parent or the other.

Translanguaging

Many of our interviewees described the linguistic environment in their homes as being mixed. Previously, we heard from Farah about why she speaks Indonesian with her children. Below, we hear from her husband, Craig, who describes how their family mix English and Bahasa Indonesia at home:

> Craig: I would say now in the household, like my wife obviously uses Indonesian with the kids a lot, but not all the time, especially if I'm there, but we use a lot of Indonesian words for common activities, so you know, it's time for a shower, clean brush your teeth, you know, eat. Or like "makan", yeah. Sometimes basic questions like, "Why?" or "What are you doing?", too. Those types of words as well, we would switch between English and Indonesian. I think part of it is just that, if I know the word and we all know it, then it becomes part of the accepted vocab and my little my vocab unfortunately is so limited that it's not wider and we had um you know, a helper that was Indonesian so that that helped a lot to enforce a certain level of Indonesian in the household.

Craig and Farah's family employ translanguaging for their everyday communication. They speak English as the main language because Craig cannot speak Indonesian well, but Farah still speaks Indonesian with the children when Craig is not around. In this case, Craig and Farah have made the decision to use more English as a family to ensure that Craig is not isolated from the conversation. Nonetheless, the whole family adds in snippets of Bahasa Indonesia when it comes to discussing daily activities. This is a tailor-made language practice that uniquely suits this family.

Talking with Friends: *We're Just Going to Ignore Him and Speak in Indonesian*

The final major group of speech partners that our ICs have are friends. Maintaining friendships with those of a similar background is crucial for ICs. This might mean that one spouse cannot understand the conversation that the other is having—for example, when Hyejeong and I speak to our Korean friends, we often speak in Korean, even if our English-speaking husbands are present. Inevitably, there will be some moments of disconnect. If Hyejeong and I were to chat to our Korean friends in English, the interaction would feel very limited. Our husbands do not mind, as they would not expect us to speak in a language that we are less comfortable with. Nonetheless, there will always be some translanguaging on our part. We often mix English and Korean together when speaking with Korean friends living in Britain or Australia. It is very important for each spouse to have their own 'safe' interactions with their friends in their most comfortable language. It can provide relief to the immigrant spouse, who is constantly dealing with the discomfort of speaking a second language in their daily life. Below, Craig describes the language practice that he and his wife adopt in relation to friends:

> Interviewer: When you, I guess, when you are around your friends, the language you guys speak is mainly English?
> Craig: That's another difficulty for me. If they want me to be in the conversation, they'll switch to English. Her friends are mostly able to speak English but there's kind of a limit and it frustrates me that I am sitting at a table with eight people and I'm forcing them to speak in English just because I can't speak their language. I mean, to be fair to them, I'm perfectly okay with this. Most of the time they'll just be like, we're just going to ignore him and speak in Indonesian, if he can pick up 5%, then fine. We're not you know, we haven't seen Farah's family in a year, we're going to just chat and perhaps they'll translate some parts and occasionally the conversation might switch to English if I'm in there.

Craig shows a very healthy attitude towards language practice with friends. He gives Farah her space to speak Indonesian. He understands the necessity of Farah having that comfortable space in which to speak Bahasa Indonesia, and he does not put pressure on them to speak in English for his sake. If Farah's friends do want him to join in the conversation they all switch to English, however. This is delicate translanguaging. Farah's friends will switch into English if they need to include him. Thus, translanguaging is an inclusive tool. Translanguaging is a social practice that can help us to build an inclusive society. This is particularly important for multilingual and multicultural societies. Translanguaging is creative and inclusive.

Otherwise, I Will Feel Like a Burden

Tony and Jane present a unique case amongst our interviewees. Although Jane is ethnically Korean, she speaks Mandarin comfortably, as she grew up in China. She speaks Mandarin with Tony and her friends. Tony has similar proficiency in Mandarin as Jane has in English, so neither feels that there is an imbalance in their languages, despite the fact that Jane's first language is Korean. Therefore, they have no problems interacting with each other's friends as they are on equal footing. Jane describes this below:

> Jane: He speaks perfect Chinese now. Actually, when we hang out with my friends, he can actually, hopefully talk to my friends, there was no language barrier.
> Interviewer: He can fit in.
> Jane: Yeah that's also very important, otherwise I will feel like a burden.

Being able to speak each other's language enables the couple to join in each other's friendship circle. This benefits their long-term relationship as they are able to share as much life experience as they can, using translanguaging practices. Jane mentions that she would 'feel like a burden' if conversations with her friends were to leave Tony out. This highlights just how beneficial it is to learn your partner's language to a high level of proficiency. Tony and Jane are an ideal case in this sense. There is no need to worry about leaving anyone out, as they are able to use both English and Mandarin proficiently.

The Language Is Fun and Dynamic and Fast Moving

ICs can truly be themselves when they are interacting with other ICs. In such cases, two or more couples interact knowing that they have dealt with similar issues, be they about language or culture. When two ICs of the same cultural backgrounds interact, the conversation can be especially compelling, as Nate pointed out:

Nate: I have another group of friends who include Tony and Jane, that's a really enjoyable language group because everything's interchangeable. The four of us don't get together that often, yeah, the language is fun and dynamic and fast moving and we can be precise. Not only is it enjoyable, but it's rare. We have other friends in Singapore, with a Chinese wife and a Western husband, where the husband doesn't speak any Chinese. The situations where the guy doesn't speak Chinese are as awkward, because if Thea and the girl start speaking Chinese about something, I can stay involved in the conversation, but the other guy can't stay involved, so do I now go and talk to him because he's not involved in this, or do I stay involved in? That can be awkward, but I guess, in a sense, no problem.

Both Nate and Tony speak English most comfortably, and Thea and Jane speak Mandarin comfortably, and all can understand both languages. Thus, when they get together, they can translanguage using English and Mandarin in a borderless manner. In doing so, they can finally share the unique hybrid language and culture that they have been using in their household. This form of translanguaging, when the other party completely understands you, builds solidarity and humour between the two parties. Nate describes these kinds of conversations as having language that is 'fun and dynamic and fast moving'. He also notes that it allows them to be 'precise'. Both Jane and Tony and Nate and Thea have done the work as couples to understand each other's cultural backgrounds. This means that when the four meet up together, there is no need to explain about British or Chinese culture, broadly speaking. This makes their conversations even more fulfilling. In comparison, if Nate meets with a Chinese-English couple in which one person does not speak Mandarin, he feels a bit awkward about which language he should use. The delicate translanguaging balance is broken when even one friend does not have the same linguistic repertoire, and this can put strain on those who do, because they are not sure how or whether to compensate.

Summary

ICs do not just need to consider how they talk with each other; there are a range of other speech partners that must be considered carefully as well. In-laws are a particular issue for Asian-Western couples, as it is important to show the right respect to Asian in-laws. It would be easy for the Western spouse to make a cultural faux pas unknowingly. Issues also arise between

Asian-Asian couples, as there are different cultural norms in each Asian country, so both spouses have to learn new politeness standards. How to talk with children also poses an issue. Although a child's brain can easily deal with multiple languages, especially when they are used naturally within the home, some parents still worry about 'confusing' their children. As such, they try to avoid speaking their first language to their child. Others have trouble with their children not knowing enough of their heritage languages. Friends are the final group of significant language partners with whom our ICs engage regularly. Friends are a reprieve for each spouse because they can speak comfortably using the language with which they are most familiar together. Time with friends is of crucial importance to ICs. Overall, all ICs face similar conflicts. The greater the differences in culture and background, the more they may struggle and the more time and effort it takes to make the relationship work. This chapter, in particular, has highlighted that Asian-Western couples face different conflicts to Western-Western couples. It is not possible to apply the same observations to all ICs. To truly understand an IC, you must first consider their cultural repertoires. Only then can you begin to understand the issues that they are navigating in their lives every day.

REFERENCE

Kiaer, J. (2023). *Language of hallyu: More than polite*. Routledge.
Kiaer, J., Morgan-Brown, J., & Choi, N. (2021). *Young children's foreign language anxiety: The case of South Korea*. Multilingual matters.

CHAPTER 5

The Language of Culture

Abstract Culture and language are inextricably linked. Culture is co-constructed through language and other symbolic systems, such as images, videos, and even social media. According to Kramsh (1988), culture can be defined as 'membership in a discourse community that shares a common social space and history, and common imagining. Even when they have left that community, its members may retain, a common system of standards for perceiving, believing, evaluating, and acting wherever they maybe. These standards are what is generally called their *culture*. Culture provides you with a way of thinking, behaving, and apprehending the world around you. We are both the actors and creators of culture. With every act of language, we both consolidate and develop what it means to belong to our respective cultures. Culture is now seen as a heterogeneous entity. We rarely belong to just one culture: we all have a unique combination of national, regional, ethnic, occupational, professional, gendered, and generational belonging. Our culture is linked to our sense of self-identity, and often provides us with legitimacy.

Culture and language are inextricably linked. Culture is co-constructed through language and other symbolic systems, such as images, videos, and even social media. According to Kramsh (1998), culture can be defined as 'membership in a discourse community that shares a common social space and history, and common imagining. Even when they have left that community, its members may retain, a common system of standards for perceiving, believing, evaluating, and acting wherever they maybe. These standards are what is generally called their *culture*. Culture provides you with a way of thinking, behaving, and apprehending the world around you. We are both the actors and creators of culture. With every act of language, we both consolidate and develop what it means to belong to our respective cultures. Culture is now seen as a heterogeneous entity. We rarely belong to just one culture: we all have a unique combination of national, regional, ethnic, occupational, professional, gendered, and generational belonging. Our culture is linked to our sense of self-identity, and often provides us with legitimacy.

For ICs, the significance of co-constructed culture is huge. Both partners in an IC couple bring their own culture to the relationship, and then the couple must work out how the two cultures can co-exist and eventually even combine, so that they can live harmoniously. The shared culture between two spouses must be resolved via negotiation rather than domination. In this way, the challenges that ICs face are not just related to the linguistics of their communication, but also the cultural context of their communication. Culture is expressed in all aspects of life. As we will see, culture can be expressed through cooking, festivals, weddings, cultural activities, gift-giving, and even finances. In negotiating these everyday occurrences, couples embark on a journey to co-construct their culture together. In this pursuit, one culture should not take centre stage. Instead, both cultures should be incorporated, at least to some extent, so that the couple construct a shared culture between them in an egalitarian manner. Coming from two different cultures can be difficult, but it can also make a couple's lives richer and more diverse. For ICs, transculturation, that is to say 'cultural transformation marked by the influx of new culture elements and the loss or alteration of existing ones' is inevitable (Merriam-Webster, n.d.). Transculturation is even further enabled due to the ubiquitous access to social media and the online world. Learning about another culture and accessing its cultural content has never been so easy.

The Landscapes of our Tables

Every table is different. How we set our tables with different dishes and beverages is unique to every household. ICs, however, have to design their table even more attentively. For Asian-Western couples, the carbohydrates of each meal may pose the greatest challenge. It is safe to say that pretty much every Asian household eats a lot of rice. In Korea, it is common to eat rice at every meal. When Hyejeong and I moved to Australia and the United Kingdom respectively, we would find meals with potato or bread lacking. Such dishes felt like appetisers, and we would subconsciously be waiting for a main meal, which would be indicated by rice. Rice is so representative of a meal that we even ask *'bab meogeosseo?'*, which literally translates to 'have you eaten rice?', as a common greeting in Korean. Thus, when landscaping the Asian table there will always be some kind of rice served, even at breakfast time. In East Asia, it is standard to eat some form of short grain sticky rice. In South Asia and the Middle East, long grain rice is more often eaten, with an emphasis on all the grains being large and separated.

The ubiquity of rice in Asian food cultures means that Asian-Western couples will all have had some form of discussion about rice. On a Western table the landscaping, involved with carbohydrates eaten at each meal varies. One might eat bread for breakfast, pasta at lunchtime, and potatoes for dinner. Thus, the Western spouse in an Asian-Western couple might end up asking, 'Why do you want to eat so much rice?' In Hyejeong's household, the table landscaping is divided. Hyejeong tends to eat in Korean style, with rice, vegetables, and a soy-based dish, whilst her husband prefers to eat a more meat-heavy diet. Their son often eats Korean food with Hyejeong, but he eats some of his father's food too. In the Kiaer household, we have a hybrid table landscape. When my husband and I spent a few months in Korea at the beginning of our marriage, he suffered from indigestion because of the amount of rice he was eating. As a compromise, we often have bread and rice at the table, and my children sometimes even eat bread and rice together—a dish that they have named 'brice'. Thus, ICs have to come up with innovative solutions to their differing dietary preferences three times a day, every day. Like linguistic and cultural change, adapting to another's dietary preferences is not an easy nor automatic process. It requires juggling and negotiation.

Food: *Chicken Curry Paella*

Food is one of our basic human needs, but this does not mean that we are content to eat just anything. Every culture has its own foods, and within that, individuals will have preferences about how they make and eat their cultural food. The close link between culture and food is the reason why food and our identity are so allied. The taste of the food you grew up with can make you feel at home, even if you are thousands of miles away. Food can provide couples with an easy way to bond, both by sharing and fusing their cultures. Fusion cooking is a perfect example of how a couple can combine each spouse's culture creatively. One of our ICs from a Punjabi-Spanish household reported making chicken curry paella as a way of combining their two cultures:

> Manny: Maybe food, we do a lot of fusion cooking, so instead of doing typical Spanish paella, we do a chicken curry paella.

Manny and Lucia combine their favourite dishes and flavours to suit both of them. Paella is a typical Spanish dish, meaning that it is familiar to Lucia. They adapt the dish to include curry to suit Manny's tastes too. They eat the dish with their children, thus reinforcing their sense of multicultural identity. Food is an important, and yet easy means, by which one can share cultural heritage with one's children. In the Kiaer household, we eat a range of foods at Christmas time to share our cultural identities. My husband has Danish blood on his side, so we eat traditional pork and red cabbage on Christmas eve. Then, we eat a traditional Christmas dinner on Christmas day, with a roast bird as the centrepiece. After, we make dumplings together. My children and their British cousins all take part. I do not insist that they make the dumplings in a traditional Korean shape; we all wrap them in whichever style we prefer. We also do not put typical fillings into our dumplings. We make prawn and ginger dumplings, and my husband even adds coriander. The usual Korean filling would be tofu and kimchi. Thus, making dumplings on Christmas day is a Korean-inspired practice that the Kiaer family adapts to suit our own personal tastes. Food provides a fantastic opportunity to fuse our cultural backgrounds together, and adaptations to flavour profiles can mean that everyone enjoys the meal.

My Idea of Healthy Food Is Western Food

Whilst food can provide an opportunity for sharing both spouses' cultural backgrounds, it can also provide a ground for conflict. Western foods and Asian foods are vastly different in terms of their ingredients and cooking methods, as Craig from New Zealand noticed when living in Indonesia with Farah, his Indonesian wife.

Interviewer: Do you remember any instance of a culturally caused misunderstanding between you two? Misunderstanding or disagreement?
Craig: Yeah, I think we've had a few. Okay, like food. I think Indonesian food is really delicious, but it's not always healthy. There have been times when I've really struggled with asking maybe her mother to try to have a healthy diet, but I realised that my idea of healthy is also the kind of food that I eat, which is Western food. I think sometimes we have these kinds of cultural assumptions.

Our eating habits are hard to break, but Craig shows clear awareness of his own biases. Even though the differences between Craig and Farah's eating habits initially surprised and frustrated him, Craig shows a strong sense of self-awareness and open mindedness, which has allowed him to move past his initial difficulties. Instead of suggesting they only eat Western food to appease his notion of healthy food, Craig compromised to be accepting of Indonesian food too. If one spouse does not like the other's food, then it is easy to take it personally. This can create problems beyond the couple too. In-laws may also feel offended if their son- or daughter-in-law will not eat their cultural food. While different generations of a family might not have the same shared interests, food is a constant that they can always bond over. This also goes for spouses and their in-laws in ICs. Making and sharing food together is an important activity that brings people together. It is a source of solidarity.

Korean Is Actually Only for Food

Food is so important that some of our participants even define the cultural ground of their household according to the type of food that they eat:

Interviewer: I know you have a hybrid mix of cultures in your household but whose cultural territory do you think you are in?
Jane: China. Chinese and Korean.
Interviewer: Can you give me some examples?
Jane: For example, especially for food, when we speak Korean, it's purely for food. I teach Tony Korean names of the food and he will also Google it. He also asked what ingredients are in it, and he also makes Korean dishes, so now he cooks Korean food better than me because he follows the exact ingredients. For me, I don't mind as long as the taste is similar. I don't use any recipes. Yeah, so Korean language is actually only for food.

> Interviewer: What's your breakfast like? Is it an English breakfast, or Korean, or Chinese breakfast?
> Jane: Actually, it's all mixed.
> Interviewer: So, you guys eat mainly Korean food and a little bit of English food, but you guys speak in Chinese.
> Jane: Yeah, we don't cook Western food at all, maybe occasionally like some steak, but in terms of cooking, he cooks all Korean, and also Thai curry. He really loves Asian food. He loves Korean food. He loves *doenjang jjigae*, *kimchi jjigae*, whatever stew yeah.

Jane is ethnically Korean, but she was born and raised in China. She speaks Mandarin with her English husband, Tony, but they have a different language for food: Korean. Food provides the opportunity for the couple to enrich their translanguaging practice by adding a third language, Korean. It is interesting, however, that Jane sees their household as being Korean, because it is quite rare for husbands to cook in Korean families. It is not so uncommon, however, in Chinese and Western cultures. I was once invited to dinner by a Chinese couple when I was studying at university, and I was shocked to see that the husband cooked dumpling soup without any help from the wife. In Korea, this would almost always be the other way around. Thus, even though Jane is Korean, they do not follow Korean norms. Instead, they make their own way, dealing with household affairs as they see fit. This shows that the couple is open-minded and flexible, designing their life to suit themselves. Jane's answer evidences that the couple share a balanced power in their relationship, and their household features collaboration and mutual respect.

Festivals: *He Doesn't Celebrate Anything*

While food might provide an easy way for couples to connect, we found that our interviewees had a harder time connecting over their festivals. We often find the most delight in our cultural festivals when we are children, perhaps this is why some of our interviewees found, to their surprise, that their spouse was relatively disinterested in their cultural festivals.

> Interviewer: Do you celebrate Chinese festivals at all at home?
> Yutong: Oh my god, he's so lazy, he doesn't celebrate anything. He's just on the sofa all the time. I tried to celebrate Chinese New Year because it's very important to me and because Paige is growing up right?

Chinese born Yutong finds her German husband's lack of interest in Chinese festivals frustrating. For Yutong, the Lunar New Year is an important festival, and it is one that she wants to pass on to her daughter, Paige. Stefan, however, does not make an effort to include Chinese festivals in their couple's shared cultural repertoire. It is clear that Yutong would like this festival to be a whole family event, perhaps because it would make the festival more poignant for their daughter too. Festivals can help to enrich a couple's relationship and build greater solidarity between them. Taking the time to learn about and be interested in your spouse's festivals is an act of care that shows them you are interested.

I'm Just Celebrating by Myself

Yiyi, another Chinese woman, describes a similar situation between herself and her Italian husband, Alonso.

> Yiyi: If I want to talk about Chinese cultural things, like every year there's so many feasts, I feel I will never be able to explain clearly to him what these feasts are and why they are so important. There are three major festivals: Spring Festival, Dragon Boat Festival, and Mid-Autumn Festival. Spring Festival, generally we cook lots and the cuisines and all have a different meaning. Fish has meaning. So, when the festival approaches, I'm very sensitive about collecting all the ingredients because it's tradition, and I have celebrated for so many years, so it's a habit. I have started to collect, to buy, to order all the things online these days. Before, I was going to the market to buy. In one trip, I would not be able to collect everything, so I would go several times. And then he feels 'What are you doing? Why do you have to be so focused on collecting this food?' He doesn't understand, that always how it is celebrated. It's not really the food itself, it's the atmosphere and the manner in which we do this thing. Mid-Autumn Festival just passed last week.
> Interviewer: What did you do on Mid-Autumn Day?
> Yiyi: If I was following the traditional way, we should have eaten moon cake, we should have looked at the moon, these kinds of activities. But living with him, we ate cake, not mooncake, but cake, and drank soft drinks. And no moon, we didn't go outside to look at the moon, we were watching TV.
> [...]
> Yiyi: Like for the Spring Festival, I prepared a lot of dishes, so it took a long time. Then he is just sitting there waiting, waiting, waiting. Sometimes he still has to work, it's not a holiday here, so he goes to school to teach and he comes back late, then he'll look at me still cooking. He says, 'Why do we

have to wait so long to eat?' And then after I have prepared everything, I feel I'm just celebrating by myself. When I start to cook there is the aroma, and so the cats are super excited they follow everywhere, and they don't sleep during the day. That is a big satisfaction.

Not being able to celebrate Chinese festivals with her partner is a source of conflict for Yiyi. Yiyi spends very long hours preparing special food for the festival and her husband's lack of appreciation makes her feel frustrated. Her cats' excitement, however, makes her feel compensated for his lack of appreciation and she continues to prepare food for the celebration. Cultural festivals are anchors to your home, and past experiences and memories. They are nostalgic and comforting. In the Kiaer family, I always make sure that we celebrate Chuseok (Autumn Festival), and even though I do not particularly love it, I always make sure to buy *songpyeon* (sweet Korean rice cakes). One year I could not find any *songpyeon* to buy, as the small Korean supermarket in Oxford had sold out, and so I wondered if I should make some myself. Ultimately, I decided not to, as my family do not love *songpyeon* either. Had there been a lot of enthusiasm from them, however, then I certainly would have.

> **Tip box:** It's fine to have individual differences about which festivals you are most enthusiastic about. It is understandable that one spouse might not feel so excited about a festival that they did not grow up with. Nonetheless, encouraging one's spouse to share their festivals and related cultural activities is an act of care. In particular, an immigrant spouse will find celebrating their cultural festivals particularly comforting.

WEDDINGS: *An Indonesian Wedding Is More about the Community*

Weddings are another issue that ICs have to negotiate. Couples must choose which cultural style they want to have to follow for their wedding, or work out how to combine the two cultures together to have a culturally-hybrid wedding. They also have to fund the travel of one or both families coming to visit. In terms of the Kiaer family, around 500 people came to our wedding in Korea, but my husband only had three guests on his side, because flying to Korea in the 1990s was so expensive. In Korea, weddings are a communal affair, so the rest of our guests were made up of my university friends and people who lived in my hometown (that is, my parents' friends). The organisation and customs of Korean weddings are different to British weddings. We had a wedding manager who told my husband to wear a different suit on the day, much to his dismay. There is no wedding gift list like there is in the West, instead guests give gifts of money. One of the family members then counts how much money each person has given and presents the couple with a box of money at the end. This was very shocking to my husband's family! Weddings can be a bit of a headache for any intercultural couple. One of our participants spoke about his experience having an Indonesian style wedding:

Interviewer: Were you aware of Indonesian culture before?
Craig: I was so ignorant. Having met her I'm sort of embarrassed to think about it now. I just wasn't aware that a Muslim girl was not going to be allowed to marry someone that wasn't Muslim. I was completely ignorant of that, I mean I knew about this culture a little bit, but...
Interviewer: Can you tell me about your wedding ceremony, did you do both?
Craig: We just did Muslim style, as we were in Indonesia.
Interviewer: I see.
Craig: And I think our compromise was we had a honeymoon with my family in Bali. There was no event, but it was sort of a chance for us to, you know, hang out together. We had a very traditional Muslim wedding in a mosque, with the reception downstairs and so I had to wear the traditional attire and we did the traditional style wedding. And my wife is the one that regrets not having a Western wedding which I think she's kind of learned about through television and popular culture. A Western wedding is more about you as a couple, whereas an Indonesian wedding is more about the community. For me, it was just interesting and fun, I think for her, she wishes we've had both.
Interviewer: Were your family part of guests as well?
Craig: They were, and it was a very much an interesting cultural exchange, because my whole family came over. My immediate family met my wife's family, and they attended the wedding and I think they just had no idea what to expect and what was going on, and obviously the two families by and large couldn't communicate with each other and then like my parents-in-law don't speak English. Luckily my brother-in-law was one of the strongest speakers in both languages, other than my wife. Yeah so, he would do a lot of the sort of emceeing, if you like.

Craig and Farah chose to have a Muslim style wedding because they were in Indonesia and that is what Farah's parents would have approved of. Nonetheless, the couple compromised to have a honeymoon with Craig's family, so that both spouses could feel like they had celebrated their marriage. The wedding ceremony seems to have taught Craig a lot about Indonesian culture. He notes that an Indonesian wedding is 'about the community', whilst a Western wedding is centred around the couple. Having realised this, Farah would have liked to have had a Western style wedding too. Therefore, although the cultural style of the wedding appears to have caused little tension between the couple, Farah ended up missing out on the 'interesting and fun' learning experience that Craig had by having a traditional Indonesian Muslim wedding. In hindsight, making the effort to have two ceremonies might have been a better idea. At the time, having two weddings likely seemed like a superfluous expense, but it is important to think about the long-term impact too. Weddings are an event that a couple experiences together once. Making sure that all parties have a fond memory to look back on and cherish will always be worth the expense in hindsight.

I Just Feel Like It's like Training a Monkey

Traditional weddings are accompanied by important formalities. While these formalities might be second nature to one spouse, they can be completely unfamiliar to the other. In the case of Han Chinese traditional weddings, it is common for the couple to go from table to table making toasts. If this is not done correctly, it is easy to lose face. In Western weddings, toasts are frivolities that centre around sharing stories, jokes, and blessings. In Chinese culture, however, toasts are about showing appropriate respect. One of our Chinese interviewees, Yutong, spoke about how she was worried about performing these toasts with her German husband:

> Yutong: When Stefan and I got together, it was good news, but also a disappointment because my parents felt like their ties with me were transformed, and I think my mother particularly had a difficult time adapting to the change, and she fought a lot with me. I'll give you an example. She wanted a really lavish wedding for us in China. And, of course, she wanted to pay for that, and you know, in China, the wedding is usually for the parents and family. The guests will largely be my parents' friends.
>
> Interviewer: Yeah.

Yutong: But, at that time, I think I was really really scared of this, like you know, all dressed up like, it's just tremendous pressure, and how do I manage Stefan, how sloppy he is, how do I manage him? And then you, you have to do all these complicated toasts around each table and say the right things. I just feel like it's like training a monkey, it's really delicate. But I would just feel like I couldn't do it, and my mother was really, really angry with me and even today, I think she's a bit resentful.

Yutong initially was worried about meeting both parties' expectations about their wedding ceremony. Her mother wanted to have a huge, lavish ceremony, while her husband wanted a small and simple ceremony. She knows what her husband is like and to have asked him to have a Chinese style ceremony was unthinkable. She ended up not having a big ceremony; but she was worried that her mother could be resentful about her not having the big Chinese wedding she had hoped for her daughter.

GIFT GIVING: *KOREANS ARE MORE THOUGHTFUL*

Gift giving can also cause problems between IC spouses. Many Asian cultures have well defined gift giving cultures. For example, in Korea, if someone gives you food in Tupperware, it is common practice to return the Tupperware with food in it. In the UK, however, it is only expected that you wash the Tupperware before returning it. One of our participants, Evelyn, who is Singaporean and married to a Korean man, noted that Korean gift giving is very thoughtful:

Evelyn: I think that the Koreans are more thoughtful. They present the present very nicely wrapped and you feel very happy when you receive the present. In Singapore, I mean when I receive present I'm also happy, it's just that Singaporeans tend to give more practical presents. Sometimes they even like just give vouchers, or they just straight up and ask you 'Aye, what do you want? I'll get you what you want', but Korean I don't think they do such thing they will just think of a person and imagine what the person would love to have, and they will get it.

In Evelyn's case, gift giving is something that enriches their relationship. She describes Singaporean gift giving culture as being very pragmatic. Even though she is always happy to receive any present, she feels that Koreans put a lot of thought into what they buy, and so she enjoys the Korean style of gift giving.

Ideology: *We Rarely Have Those Discussions Now*

While a couple might be receptive to each other's cultures, that does not mean that they never face ideological clashes. Although we all have our own political views, they are often culturally influenced. For example, there is strong support for the style of government in China, while many outside of mainland China disapprove of it. Even couples that are aware of each other's cultural activities well might clash over these bigger ideological issues.

> Tony: And we, but we rarely have those discussions now, because we know that it's not good for us to do it necessarily. There was a point in time where you are sometimes tempted to raise something, if it's in the news, and we talked about it, but the chances of that turning into a confrontation was quite high, so we just don't really do it that much anymore. Different perspectives on team management or dealing with the politics and in an office, for example, but it's never triggered by linguistic reasons. It can't be pinned upon the language that we use, it's more about just differences in experience and differences in perspective.

We previously discussed Tony and Jane being very open and flexible about each other's cultures. Tony and Jane speak Mandarin at least 90% of the time, even though they can both speak English, and Tony has learnt to cook a lot of Korean food. Thus, the couple appear to have a good mutual cultural understanding. When it comes to matters of politics, they cannot always agree on the best way to do things. They thus avoid talking about such topics because they are likely to get into arguments about them. ICs share a lot, but some things just cannot be carried over. Each spouse will have different opinions that have been formed on different foundations. Part of an IC constructing their communication involves deciding what not to talk about. In the Kiaer family, for example, I rarely talk about Korean politics because there is too much to explain to have a satisfying conversation. Being on the same page does not mean that a couple needs to share and agree on everything. For me, there are some parts of British humour that I will simply never understand. ICs need to respect that some things simply will not be understood, so that they can move forward in acknowledgement of their differences.

He Wouldn't Expect Me to Like, You Know, Serve him and Take Care of Him

Yutong and Stefan are the opposite to Tony and Jane. We previously discussed how Stefan had little understanding or enthusiasm for Chinese cultural activities, but when it comes to ideology and navigating the world, the two get on very well:

> Yutong: And also, I think the good thing about him being German is that he doesn't have so much ego, you know, like Asian 'face', like he doesn't care so much. He wouldn't be so offended if I say critical things to him. This is a stereotype, but I feel like Asian men sometimes have a more delicate feelings in that regard, but he's just not that sensitive. A stereotypical Chinese male partner sometimes feels threatened by a strong wife. For example, now, my husband doesn't have a job, but he doesn't feel like it's very damaging to his ego. It doesn't make him feel uncomfortable, it doesn't make him lose his confidence. Just being a stay-at-home dad, that's totally fine for him. So, that really works well for our relationship and, I guess he has low expectation for me as a wife. Like he's very low maintenance, like he wouldn't expect me to like, you know, serve him take care of him.

Yutong likes the fact that Stefan does not worry about losing 'face' because he did not grow up in that kind of culture. He admits his mistakes and there is no issue of 'ego'. Stefan doesn't mind being wrong and he also doesn't mind that she has a powerful job while he is not working. Yutong likes that he doesn't feel threatened by having a strong wife, and he does not expect her to serve him. In this way, Yutong and Stefan's relationship is enriched by its intercultural nature, allowing the pair to exist on an equal footing. In this instance, we see how the flexibility of ICs has dynamic benefits. Yutong and Stefan are emancipated from the cultural stereotypes of each other's cultures. Were she to have married a Chinese man, then Yutong might have had to take on more of the household work. As she is married to a German man, she can forgo Chinese stereotypes of her gender. In this way, IC's relationships are dynamic and flexible in way that monocultural couple's might not be.

Let Me Remind you, I'm Not a Mail Order Bride

Although Yutong feels that she has had a positive experience with Stefan when it comes to household labour, Aliyah has not had the same experience with her Australian husband, Colin. The two clash over household chores and raising children. Aliyah works and manages all the household and child raising tasks, which she feels is quite unfair:

> Aliyah: One of the things that has come up for me recently is, and it's really bothering me, I asked him this the other day, 'Would you behave like the way you're behaving if you are married to a Caucasian woman? In the back of your mind, you have some sort of expectation that I should be subservient and do everything. Let me remind you I'm not a mail order bride.' I think Colin has many personas and I think you know, and I think that was one of the things I was attracted to, but I feel like you know, sometimes his prejudice upbringing seeps. I deeply believe his relationship to a partner who is Caucasian would be very different, that he would be raising a child very differently. I do. So recently I confronted him. I cook, I clean, I look after Rose, I'm trying to do my research, I'm trying to prepare for my classes. I need you to come in halfway. I have a clean sink at 8 pm and then, when you come at 8 pm, you eat and you do everything, and you leave a sink full of dishes. I'm always cleaning and, you know.

Issues with household labour have become so extreme that Aliyah has begun to wonder whether Colin's racially prejudiced upbringing is to blame. She feels that Colin expects her to manage all the household labour as he puts in very little effort to help. This can be a big issue in all relationships, intercultural or not. However, Aliyah wonders if the Western stereotype of Asian women being subservient, meek housewives is influencing Colin's behaviour. Thus, the issue is not just about the labour divide, but also about culture and perceptions.

It Always Helps to Remind Me that There's Another Way to Think

Being from different cultures and endeavouring to blend the two allows for reflection on your own culture and the assumptions you make. There is another way to think and there is another way to be, as Craig has become aware of:

> Interviewer: How does the fact that you're a bilingual cross-cultural couple influence your relationship?
> Craig: I think it keeps it interesting and challenging. I think certain personalities are attracted to people from different cultures, because it helps you to reflect on your own assumptions and cultures. And at least from my

perspective, it always helps to remind me that there's another way to think and there's another way to be that's just different to my own and that's something you have to have at the forefront I think, otherwise you your relationship will end in tears because you're trying to push for your own cultural position.

Craig' response highlights that belonging to an IC is actually an opportunity to learn. If you are open-minded, you open yourself up to a realm of new knowledge and new understandings about the world. Craig also illustrates that pushing your own culture onto another is a stifling act that will ultimately have negative consequences on a relationship. Even if an idea feels familiar or strange upon first encounter, it is better to take a step back and think about the cultural context of the idea, before reacting.

I don't Even Feel that we Are from Different Contexts

Over time, couples grow together, finding a comfortable place in their relationship. Intercultural relationships are dynamic, so there will always be something to negotiate, but as time passes, these issues become less serious. Alonso noted that he did not feel his wife was from a different context to him because he knows her very well, after being married for many years:

> Interviewer: Do you think that the fact that you guys are a multicultural couple has an influence on your relationship in any way?
> Alonso: I don't even feel that we are from different contexts. So, at the moment, Yiyi is just my wife as she is, she can come from China, from Italy, from Germany, from the moon, and it will be the same.

Although there is always the other cultural part of a spouse that it will take a lifetime or more to understand, it is not necessary for one to understand everything about their spouse to feel close to them. First, one understands their spouse on a personal level, and then gradually gets to know them on a cultural level. Alonso is clearly very personally close to his wife Yiyi. He feels that he knows her well enough that she could be from anywhere. Though this could be a surprising statement because cultural background is so important, Alonso's statement highlights how comfortable he is with his wife and alludes to unconditional love.

FINANCE: *WE ARE ON A MORE EQUAL FOOTING*

How to manage finances is a challenge that all couples face, regardless of whether they are intercultural or not. However, different countries have different societal norms about sharing finances, and so dealing with finance as an intercultural couple can be very tricky. Nonetheless, there can also be opportunity to break away from the gender norms related to finance, as one of our Korean participants, John, found out with his Singaporean partner, Charlie:

> John: I think it's fantastic in terms of finance, because if I married a Korean woman then they most likely would have stopped working, and it would be just me working and supporting the family. Charlie has never thought in that way. When I was working here in a local company, my English wasn't very good. Charlie's income was good. In Korea, when you go out dating, you are expected to pay for everything as the man. But, in Singapore, it's different. We are on a more equal footing, in terms of our finance, which is so great.

In Korea, it is still common for men to be the main breadwinners of the household. When moving to Singapore, John feared that he would have to shoulder the burden of making money, even though he is not fluent in English, and he has never lived there before. He quickly found out that this was not the case. Charlie was happy to work and make money for the family. She is also happy to split payments with him. In this way, being in an intercultural couple has freed John from the financial burden that he might have faced in Korea. Intercultural couples are given the gift of flexibility. They are free from having to adhere to just one society's social conventions. Although it can be tricky to navigate initially, once a couple figure it out, they often find their relationship is quite convenient.

SUMMARY

Language is often the least of an IC's troubles. Language is a logical and pragmatic issue for ICs that is about working out what your partner means. It can be frustrating, but it is likely not enough to break a couple. Cultural clashes, however, are serious. Culture defines a large part of what we see as morally and ethically correct. It sets our expectations for how life should be. For this reason, ICs have to make a lot of sacrifices and compromises. They are constantly developing a hybrid transcultural way of living together, in a tug of war to balance out their differences. If the balance swings too far towards one culture, then issues can arise. If one spouse does not show interest in the other's culture, then the other spouse might feel that they are not being paid attention or cared for. Many studies explore the linguistic side of ICs, but this chapter serves to remind us that culture is just as, if not more, important than language.

Reference

Kramsch, C. (1998). *Language and Culture*. Oxford: Oxford University Press

Merriam-Webster. (n.d.). Transculturation. In *Merriam-Webster.com dictionary*. Retrieved November 17, 2022, from https://www.merriam-webster.com/dictionary/transculturation.

Epilogue

The Ignorant Schoolmaster by Jacques Rancière (trans. Kristin Ross, 1999) describes the story of Joseph Jacotot, a lecturer in French literature, and his experience teaching French to a group of Flemish students who do not speak any of the language. With no shared language, Jacotot looks for anything that they might have in common; what he finds is a bilingual edition of the novel, *Telemaque*. Left to themselves, the students learn French through repetition and recitation of the novel. The novel questions the existential necessity of the teacher and how teaching can either be enslaving or emancipating, depending on whether learning is one directional (teacher to student) or two directional (teacher to student and student to teacher). The story of Joseph Jacotot is not so different to the experiences of our intercultural couples. Although our ICs may have shared some commonality to begin with, they are still exposed to their differences on a more fine-grained level as time goes on. They may start with little or no understanding of their partner's language and culture, and then, gradually and intuitively, they begin to learn. This is a life-long journey, requiring constant reflection and negotiation. Crucially, there is no one-directional teacher–student relationship when it comes to ICs. Both partners learn from each other, thus developing shared language and cultural practices. How an IC grows and develops over time changes case by case. The ways in which they manage their intercultural issues change day by day. ICs embark on a lifelong journey of getting to know each other, adapting to new situations and findings dynamically and innovatively along the way.

References

Abela, A., Piscopo, S., & Vella, S. (2020). Understanding love relationships in a global context: Supporting couples across cultures. In *Couple relationships in a global context* (pp. 3–17). Springer. https://doi.org/10.1007/978-3-030-37712-0_1

Ahn, H. (2017). English as a discursive and social communication resource for contemporary S. Koreans. In C. Jenks & J. W. Lee (Eds.), *Korean Englishes in transnational contexts* (pp. 157–179). Palgrave Macmillan.

Amrith, S. S. (2014). Migration and health in southeast Asian history. *The Lancet (British edition), 384*(9954), 1569–1570.

Baxter, L. A. (1987). Symbols of relationship identity in relationship cultures. *Journal of Social & Personal Relationships, 4*(3), 261–280.

Baxter, L. A. (2004). A tale of two voices: Relational dialectics theory. *Journal of Family Communication, 4*(3/4), 181–192.

Baxter, L. A., & Montgomery, B. M. (1996). *Relating: Dialogues and dialectics*. Guilford Press.

Berg-Cross, L. (2001). *Couples therapy*. Hawthorne.

Bhugun, D. (2017). Intercultural parenting in Australia. *The Family Journal, 25*(2), 187–195. https://doi.org/10.1177/1066480717697688

Bhugun, D. (2019). *Intercultural parenting and relationships: Challenges and rewards* (1st ed.). Springer International Publishing. https://doi.org/10.1007/978-3-030-14060-1

Brahic, B. (2013). The politics of bi-nationality in couple relationships: A case study of European bi-national couples in Manchester. *Journal of Comparative Family Studies, 44*(6), 699–714. https://doi.org/10.3138/jcfs.44.6.699

Bratter, J. L., & King, R. B. (2008). "But will it last?": Marital instability among interracial and same-race couples. *Family Relations, 57*(2), 160–171.

Brummett, E. A., & Steuber, K. R. (2015). To reveal or conceal?: Privacy management processes among interracial romantic partners. *Western Journal of Communication, 79*(1), 22–44.

Bustamante, R. M., Nelson, J. A., Henriksen, R. C., & Monakes, S. (2011). Intercultural couples: Coping with culture-related stressors. *The Family Journal, 19*(2), 154–164. https://doi.org/10.1177/1066480711399723

Bystydzienski, J. M. (2011). *Intercultural couples: Crossing boundaries, negotiating difference.* New York University Press.

Canagarajah, S. (2011). Translanguaging in the classroom: Emerging issues for research and pedagogy. *Applied Linguistics Review, 2*(1), 1–28.

Canagarajah, A. S. (2013). *Translingual practice global Englishes and cosmopolitan relations.* Routledge.

Canagarajah, S., & Dovchin, S. (2019). The everyday politics of translingualism as a resistant practice. *International Journal of Multilingualism, 16*(2), 127–144.

Cerchiaro, F. (2017). 'In the name of the children': Mixed couples' parenting analysed through their naming practices. *Identities, 26*(1), 51–68. https://doi.org/10.1080/1070289x.2017.1353314

Chi, Y.-F. (2014). *Multilingual couples' disagreement: Taiwanese partners and their foreign spouses.* University of London.

Constable, N. (2003). *Romance on a global stage: Pen pals, virtual ethnography, and "mail order" marriages.* University of California Press. http://www.jstor.org/stable/10.1525/j.ctt1pnr50

Constable, N. (Ed.). (2005). *Cross-border marriages: Gender and mobility in transnational Asia.* University of Pennsylvania Press. http://www.jstor.org/stable/j.ctt3fhv66

Coupland, N., Wiemann, J. M., & Giles, H. (1991). Talk as "problem" and communication as "miscommunication": An integrative analysis. In N. Coupland, J. M. Wiemann, & H. Giles (Eds.), *"Miscommunication" and problematic talk* (pp. 1–17). SAGE Publication.

Dervin, F. (2013). Do intercultural couples "see culture everywhere"? *Civilisations, 62,* 131–148. https://doi.org/10.4000/civilisations.3352

Dewaele, J.-M. (2008). The emotional weight of I love you in multilinguals' languages. *Journal of Pragmatics, 40*(10), 1753–1780. https://doi.org/10.1016/j.pragma.2008.03.002

Dewaele, J.-M. (2013). *Emotions in multiple languages.* Palgrave Macmillan.

Dewaele, J.-M. (2015). From obscure echo to language of the heart: Multilinguals' language choices for (emotional) inner speech. *Journal of Pragmatics, 87,* 1–17. https://doi.org/10.1016/j.pragma.2015.06.014

Dewaele, J.-M. (2016). Thirty shades of offensiveness: L1 and LX English users' understanding, perception and self-reported use of negative emotion-laden words. *Journal of Pragmatics, 94,* 112–127. https://doi.org/10.1016/j.pragma.2016.01.009

Dewaele, J.-M. (2018a). Pragmatic challenges in the communication of emotions in intercultural couples. *Intercultural Pragmatics, 15*(1), 29–55. https://doi.org/10.1515/ip-2017-0029

Dewaele, J.-M. (2018b). Why the dichotomy 'L1 versus LX user' is better than 'native versus non-native speaker'. *Applied Linguistics, 39*(2), 236–240.

Dewaele, J.-M., & Salomidou, L. (2017). Loving a partner in a foreign language. *Journal of Pragmatics, 108,* 116–130. https://doi.org/10.1016/j.pragma.2016.12.009

Epp, A. M., Schau, H. J., & Price, L. L. (2014). The role of brands and mediating technologies in assembling long-distance family practices. *Journal of Marketing, 78*(3), 81–101.

Falicov, C. J. (1995). Cross-cultural marriages. In *Clinical handbook of couple therapy* (pp. 231–246). Guilford.

Foreign Service Institute. (n.d.). *Foreign Language Training* (no date) *U.S. Department of State.* Available at: https://www.state.gov/foreign-language-training/. Accessed November 17, 2022.

Fu, X., & Heaton, T. B. (2000). Status exchange in intermarriage among Hawaiians, Japanese, Filipinos and Caucasians in Hawaii: 1983–1994. *Journal of Comparative Family Studies, 31*(1), 45–61. https://doi.org/10.3138/jcfs.31.1.45

García, O., & Leiva, C. (2014). Theorising and enacting translanguaging for social justice. In A. Blackledge & A. Creese (Eds.), *Heteroglossia as practice and pedagogy* (pp. 199–216). Springer.

García, O., & Li, W. (2014). *Translanguaging: Language, bilingualism and education.* Palgrave Macmillan. http://ezlibproxy1.ntu.edu.sg/login?url=http://search.ebscohost.com/login.aspx?direct=true&db=cat00103a&AN=ntu.a1295037&site=eds-live&scope=site

Gibbons, J. (1987). *Code-mixing and code choice: A Hong Kong case study.* Multilingual Matters.

Gumperz, J. C. (1982). *Discourse strategies.* Cambridge University Press.

Gumperz, J. J., & Gumperz, J. C. (1981). Ethnic differences in communicative style. In C. Ferguson & S. Heath (Eds.), *Language in the USA* (pp. 430–445). Cambridge University Press.

Hirschmann, R. (2021). *Estimated number of Asian immigrants in Singapore in 2020, by country of origin, Statista.* Available at: https://www.statista.com/statistics/692951/asian-immigrant-stock-of-singapore-by-country-of-origin/. Accessed November 17, 2022.

Hirschmann, R. (2022). *Number of immigrants in Singapore from 2005 to 2020, Statista.* Available at: https://www.statista.com/statistics/698035/singapore-number-of-immigrants/. Accessed November 17, 2022.

Iwakabe, S. (2019). Working through shame with an intercultural couple in Japan: Transforming negative emotional interactions and expanding positive emotional resources. *Journal of Clinical Psychology, 75*(11), 2060–2071. https://doi.org/10.1002/jclp.22864

Kalmijn, M. (1998). Intermarriage and homogamy: Causes, patterns, trends. *Annual Review of Sociology, 24*, 395–421.

Kashyap, L. (2020). Changing couple relationships in India. In *Couple relationships in a global context* (pp. 71–83). Springer. https://doi.org/10.1007/978-3-030-37712-0_5

Kiaer, J. (2021). *Pragmatic particles: Findings from Asian languages*. Bloomsbury. (Bloomsbury studies in theoretical linguistics).

Kiaer, J. (2023a). *Language of hallyu: More than polite*. Routledge.

Kiaer, J. (2023b). *Multimodal communication in young multilingual children: Learning beyond words*. Multilingual Matters.

Kim, E. (2006). Reasons and motivations for code-mixing and code-switching. *EFL, 4*(Spring 2006), 43–61.

Kline, S. L., Horton, B., & Zhang, S. (2008). Communicating love: Comparisons between American and east Asian university students. *International Journal of Intercultural Relations, 32*(3), 200–214. https://doi.org/10.1016/j.ijintrel.2008.01.006

Kramsch, C. J. (1998). *Language and culture*. Oxford University Press. (Oxford introductions to language study).

Kroeber, A. L., & Kluckhohn, C. (1963). *Culture: A critical review of concepts and definitions* (1st Vintage ed.). Vintage Books.

Kull, A. (2018). *Perceived communication of emotion in intercultural Estonian-Australian couples*. The University of Queensland.

Lawton, B., Foeman, A., & Braz, M. (2013). Interracial couples' conflict styles on educational issues. *Journal of Intercultural Communication Research, 42*(1), 35–53. https://doi.org/10.1080/17475759.2012.711766

Le Gall, J., & Meintel, D. (2015). Cultural and identity transmission in mixed couples in Quebec, Canada. *The Annals of the American Academy of Political and Social Science, 662*(1), 112–128. https://doi.org/10.1177/0002716215602705

Lee, J. (2005). Korean-English bilinguals (KEB) vs. English monolinguals (EM): Language and international marriage partnership. In *The 4th International Symposium on Bilingualism*.

Lee, J. W. (2022). Translanguaging research methodologies. *Research Methods in Applied Linguistics, 1*(1), 100004.

Lee, J., & Bean, F. D. (2004). America's changing color lines: Immigration, race/ethnicity, and multiracial identification. *Annual Review of Sociology, 30*, 221–242.

REFERENCES

Lee, J. W., & Canagarajah, S. (2021). Translingualism and world Englishes. *Bloomsbury World Englishes Volume 1: Paradigms, 1*, 99.

Leeds-Hurwitz, W. (2009). Ambiguity as a solution to the "problem" of intercultural weddings. In T. Karis & K. Killian (Eds.), *Intercultural couples: Exploring diversity in intimate relationships* (pp. 167–187). Routledge.

Li, W. (2011). Moment analysis and translanguaging space: Discursive construction of identities by multilingual Chinese youth in Britain. *Journal of Pragmatics, 43*(5), 1222–1235.

Li, W. (2018). Translanguaging as a practical theory of language. *Applied Linguistics, 39*(1), 9–30. https://doi.org/10.1093/applin/amx039

Mandela, N. (2011). *Nelson Mandela by himself: The authorised book of quotations*. Macmillan.

Menzies, F. (2015). *Paralanguage across cultures, include-empower.com*. Available at: https://cultureplusconsulting.com/2015/04/16/paralanguage-across-cultures/. Accessed November 17, 2022.

Merriam-Webster. (n.d.). Transculturation. In *Merriam-Webster.com dictionary*. Retrieved November 17, 2022, from https://www.merriam-webster.com/dictionary/transculturation.

Milroy, L., & Gordon, M. J. (2003). *Sociolinguistics: Method and interpretation*. Blackwell.

Molina, B., Estrada, D., & Burnett, J. A. (2004). Cultural communities: Challenges and opportunities in the creation of "happily ever after" stories of intercultural couplehood. *The Family Journal, 12*(2), 139–147. https://doi.org/10.1177/1066480703261962

Moyer, M. G. (1997). One speaker, two languages: Cross-disciplinary perspectives on code-switching. *Journal of Linguistic Anthropology, 7*(2), 237–239. https://doi.org/10.1525/jlin.1997.7.2.237

Muysken, P. (2000). *Bilingual speech. A typology of code-switching*. Cambridge University Press.

Myers-Scotton, C. (1993). *Duelling languages: Grammatical structure in codeswitching*. Oxford University Press.

Pavlenko, A. (2005). *Emotions and multilingualism*. Cambridge University Press.

Pietikäinen, K. S. (2016). Misunderstandings and ensuring understanding in private ELF talk. *Applied Linguistics, 39*(2), 188–212. https://doi.org/10.1093/applin/amw005

Piller, I. (2002). *Bilingual couples talk: The discursive construction of hybridity*. John Benjamins.

Piller, I. (2007). Cross-cultural communication in intimate relationships. In H. Kotthoff & H. Spencer-Oatey (Eds.), *Intercultural communication* (pp. 341–359). Mouton de Gruyter.

Piller, I. (2009). I always wanted to marry a cowboy: Bilingual couples, language, and desire. In T. Karis & K. Killian (Eds.), *Intercultural couples: Exploring diversity in intimate relationships* (pp. 53–70). Taylor & Francis.

Piller, I. (2017). *Intercultural communication: A critical introduction* (2nd ed.). Edinburgh University Press.

Quah, S. R. (2003). Ethnicity and parenting styles among Singapore families. *Marriage and Family Review, 35*(3), 63–83.

Rancière, J., & Ross, K. (1999). *The ignorant schoolmaster: Five lessons in intellectual emancipation.* Stanford University Press.

Rogan, D., Piacentini, M., & Hopkinson, G. (2018). Intercultural household food tensions: A relational dialectics analysis. *European Journal of Marketing, 52*(12), 2289–2311. https://doi.org/10.1108/ejm-10-2017-0778

Rosenblatt, P. C. (2011). A systems theory analysis of intercultural couple relationships. In *Intercultural couples* (pp. 24–41). Routledge.

Scollon, R., & Scollon, S. W. (2001). Discourse and intercultural communication. In D. Schiff & H. Hamilton (Eds.), *The handbook of discourse analysis* (pp. 538–547). Blackwell Wiley.

Scollon, R., Scollon, S. W., & Jones, R. H. (2012). *Intercultural communication: A discourse approach.* John Wiley & Sons, Incorporated. http://ebookcentral.proquest.com/lib/unimelb/detail.action?docID=822409

Seshadri, G., & Knudson-Martin, C. (2013). How couples manage interracial and intercultural differences: Implications for clinical practice. *Journal of Marital and Family Therapy, 39*(1), 43–58. https://doi.org/10.1111/j.1752-0606.2011.00262.x

Shenhav, S., Campos, B., & Goldberg, W. A. (2016). Dating out is intercultural. *Journal of Social and Personal Relationships, 34*(3), 397–422. https://doi.org/10.1177/0265407516640387

Skowroński, D., Ying Cherie, T. S., Fernandez, T. M., Fong Tay Danx, D., Ho Wen Wan, M., & Waszyńska, K. (2014). Introductory analysis of factors affecting intercultural couples in the context of Singapore. *Studia Edukacyjne, 30*, 263–268. https://doi.org/10.14746/se.2014.30.15

Stępkowska, A. (2021). Identity in the bilingual couple: Attitudes to language and culture. *Open Linguistics, 7*(1), 223–234. https://doi.org/10.1515/opli-2021-0020

Takigawa, Y. (2010). *Language expertise as a source of dispute in bilingual couple talk.* Temple University. http://hdl.handle.net/20.500.12613/2502

Tan, C. L.-L. (2016). *Sarong party girls.* HarperCollins.

Tannen, D. (1986). *That's not what I meant!* Ballantine Books.

Taweekuakulkit, N. (2005). *Thai-north American intercultural marriage in the United States: A qualitative study of conflict from Thai wives' perspectives.* Wayne State University.

Tay, M. W. J. (1989). Code switching and code mixing as a communicative strategy in multilingual discourse. *World Englishes, 8*(3), 407–417. https://doi.org/10.1111/j.1467-971X.1989.tb00678.x

Tien, N. C. (2013). *Communication and relationships of intercultural/multilingual couples: Cultural and language differences.* University of Colorado.

Zhang, Y., & Van Hook, J. (2009). Marital dissolution among interracial couples. *Journal of Marriage and Family, 71*(1), 95–107.

Zhu, H. (2019). *Exploring intercultural communication: Language in action.* Routledge.

Index

A
Affection, 12, 30, 65–66
Anger, 16, 17, 29, 30, 57–62, 65
Asian-Asian couple, v, vi, 2, 17, 97
Asian-Western couple, v, vi, 2, 3, 17, 30, 54, 72, 96, 97, 100, 101

B
Bahasa Indonesia, 19, 58, 67, 89, 93, 94

C
Cantonese, 21, 24, 25, 51
Children, v, 2, 4, 5, 10–12, 19–21, 25, 28, 30, 58, 67–69, 71–76, 81–93, 97, 101, 102, 104, 112
Chinese dialects, 21
Code-mixing, 8–9
Code-switching, 8–9, 16, 27
Conflict, 2, 6, 10–14, 26, 31, 47, 58–62, 66, 80, 81, 92, 97, 102, 106
Cross-cultural communication, 7, 41
Culture, v, vi, 2–5, 7, 11–14, 19, 26–29, 31, 43–46, 67, 69, 70, 73, 74, 76, 78, 79, 81–83, 85–89, 91–92, 95–97, 99–115, 117

E
Emotional communication, 6, 15, 16

F
Festival, 7, 27, 31, 100, 104–106
Finance, 31, 100, 114
French, 18, 21, 45–47, 63, 117

G
Gift giving, 100, 109

H
Home, 5, 21, 23, 25, 26, 44, 45, 47, 48, 67–69, 71–74, 89–91, 93, 97, 102, 104, 106, 111

I

Ideology, 10, 15, 31, 110–113
Immigrant spouse, 5, 26, 30, 40, 48, 56, 84, 94, 106
In-law communication, 79
Intercultural communication, 2, 3, 7, 29
Intercultural couple, v, vi, 1–4, 7, 9–14, 16, 17, 26, 27, 29, 40, 47, 56, 72, 75, 88, 107, 114, 117
Intercultural relationship, 1–31, 113
Intimacy, 1, 56, 63
Italian, 21, 49–51, 60, 65–66, 105

J

Jokes, 2, 56, 65, 67, 82, 108

K

Korean, 3, 9, 16–18, 22, 23, 25, 41–45, 48, 49, 51–54, 60, 62, 64, 66, 68, 72–76, 78, 80, 84, 85, 89, 90, 94, 95, 101–104, 106, 107, 109, 110, 114

L

Language choice, 6, 14–16, 30, 47, 56, 77

M

Malay, 18, 19, 21, 23, 25, 63
Mandarin, 18–25, 42, 43, 49–51, 53, 54, 59–65, 68, 69, 92, 95, 96, 104, 110

N

Negotiation, vi, 3, 4, 27, 29–31, 40–54, 59, 62, 66, 100, 101, 117

P

Piedmontese, 21
Punjabi, 21, 102

R

Respect, 30, 40, 43–46, 56, 73, 76, 78, 79, 81, 96, 104, 108, 110

S

Singapore, v, vi, 2, 3, 10, 19–25, 45, 47–49, 63, 72, 78, 79, 87–90, 92, 96, 109, 114
Slovak, 18, 45–47, 61–63, 79–81, 90, 91
Spanish, 4, 20, 21, 23, 69, 75, 102
Swear, 57, 61–62

T

Tamil, 19
Technology, vi, 29, 62, 72, 83–85
Translanguaging, v, 5, 8–9, 26–28, 30, 31, 40, 43–48, 52–54, 57–61, 63–67, 69, 70, 77, 91, 93–96, 104
Translanguaging competence, 57–58
Translanguaging space, 5

W

Wider family, v, 2, 4, 11, 29, 30, 58, 71–97

Printed by Printforce, United Kingdom